Lost in the Rhythm

AF326839

Keepin' the F

Matt Stokes
Lost in th

Rea
No Way Bac

Passion and Ecstasy of a T

Artist's Informatio

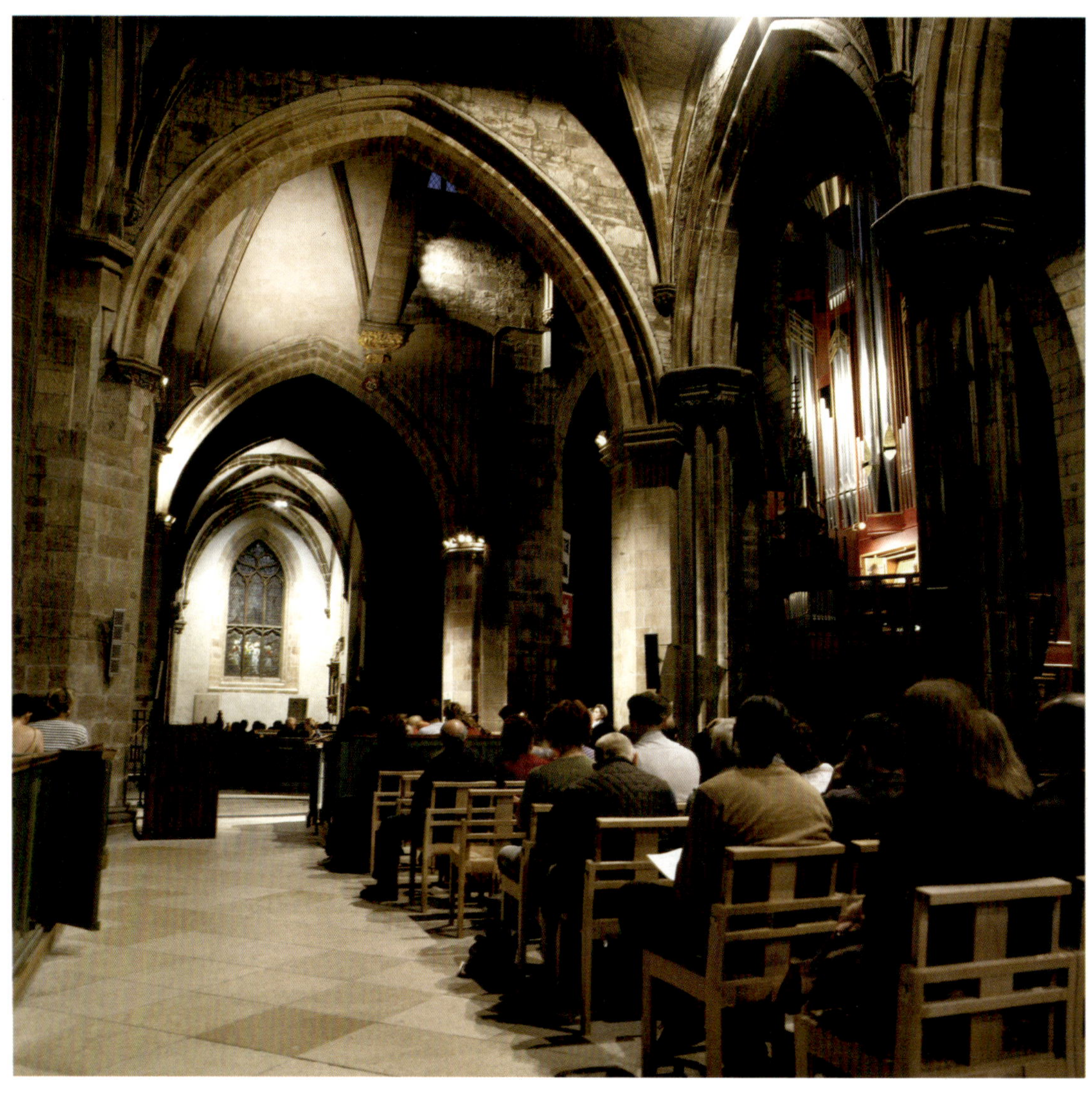

Sacred Selections, performance at St Giles' Cathedral, Edinburgh.
24 August 2006.

Foreword

Sarah Munro

There has been a significant change in the global environment of art and its production. Not only are the possibilities for art greater and more diverse than ever, but also the world we inhabit is more complex and unpredictable. A world increasingly characterised by the privatisation of the public realm, a reduction in the possibilities for public debate, mounting apathy with traditional political routes and a growing sense of insecurity for almost all peoples, cannot be isolated from the cultural production of those living within it.

'Art when it is more than a luxury commodity relates to the discourse in what remains of the public sphere. It contributes to that discourse, or tries to create the ground on which it can happen. How we imagine the public sphere as a society is vital to how we see ourselves and our collective potentiality and if we lose the idea of the public sphere entirely, then we lose our potential for acting together.'[1]

The power of art resides in its power of storytelling, of sense making, of questioning, of restoring meaning. But, perhaps the greatest potential of art lies in the very process through which the artist – in intimate, personal and allusive ways – enables us to begin to imagine alternatives. Unlike many artists steeped in modernist tradition and its conventions, Matt Stokes is part of a newer generation of artists whose extended praxis involves a broader investigation of our culture.

Stokes' practice is embedded in an anthropological enquiry of the broader subcultural movements that bring people together. His methodologies often lie in the development of collaborative and live elements, which arise through investigations into a range of factional and disparate communities connected to particular environs. By way of this process, he utilises collaboration as a space for negotiation and appreciation of individual and group identities.

His interest in collectivity, in creating connections between a location and an activity, is often anchored by music and its ability to shape both lifestyles and beliefs. 'For those who love music, it remains as a fixed point of reference… a source of reconciliation, exhilaration, and hope which never fails.'[2] Via his archaeological 'digs' into the ephemera of underground cultures such as the Northern Soul scene and Rave

1   Charles Esche. Interview with Charles Esche by Pelin Tan, 2005, www.translate.eipcp.net.
2   Storr, Anthony, **Music and the Mind**, Collins, 1992

phenomenon, he has, like a cultural alchemist, created significant new works that transform our understanding in new ways.

This approach has partly evolved from **Real Arcadia**; an expansive and evolving project based on the history of a defunct Acid House organisation from the Lake District, and was extended through his film works **Long After Tonight** and **Cipher**, and the ongoing series of performances **Sacred Selections**, all of which are represented within this publication.

Lost in the Rhythm and the exhibition that led to its inception, *Pills to Purge Melancholy* (Collective Gallery, 2006) offers the first opportunity for the diverse and engaging work of Matt Stokes to be brought together and explored in depth.

Collective are extremely grateful to Matthew Collin, Momus and Rob Tufnell for their text contributions, Jon Bewley and Jonty Tarbuck for their editorial support, and Art Editions North for their collaboration. However, the most important contributor has been the artist himself whose commitment to both this publication, and the exhibition that preceded it, has made the experience so worthwhile.

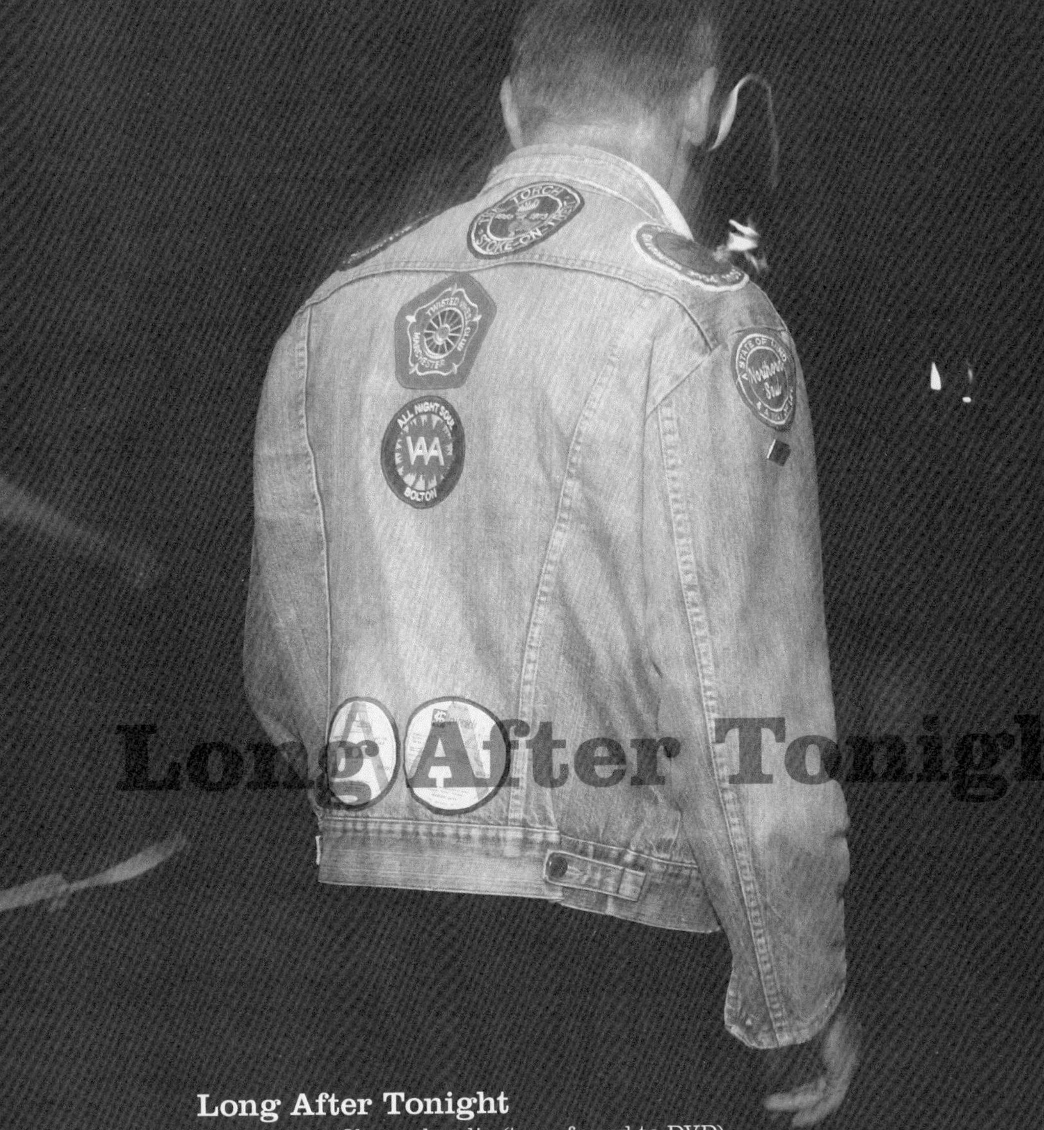

Long After Tonight
Super 16mm film and audio (transferred to DVD)
2005
Duration 6 minutes 45 seconds

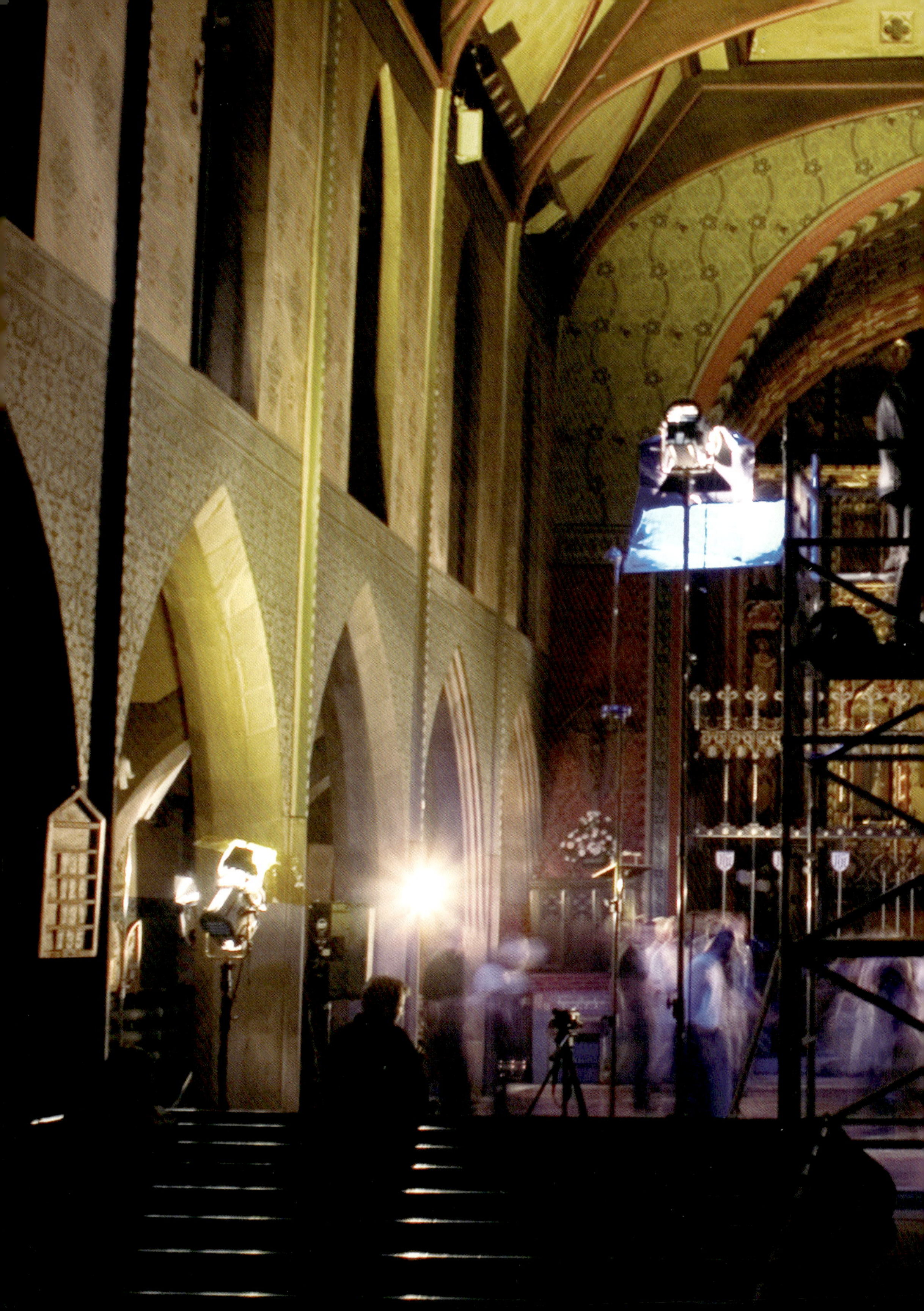

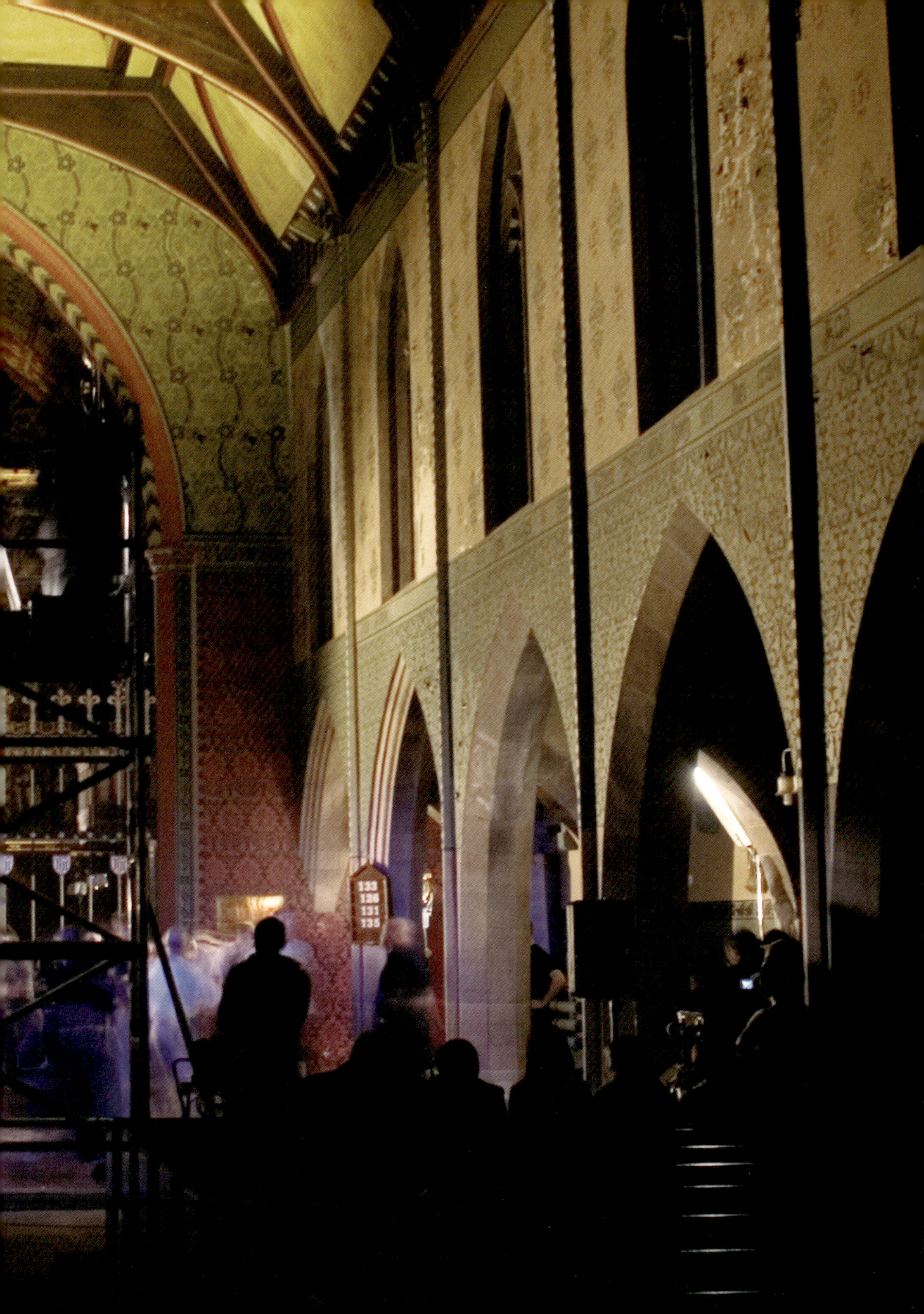

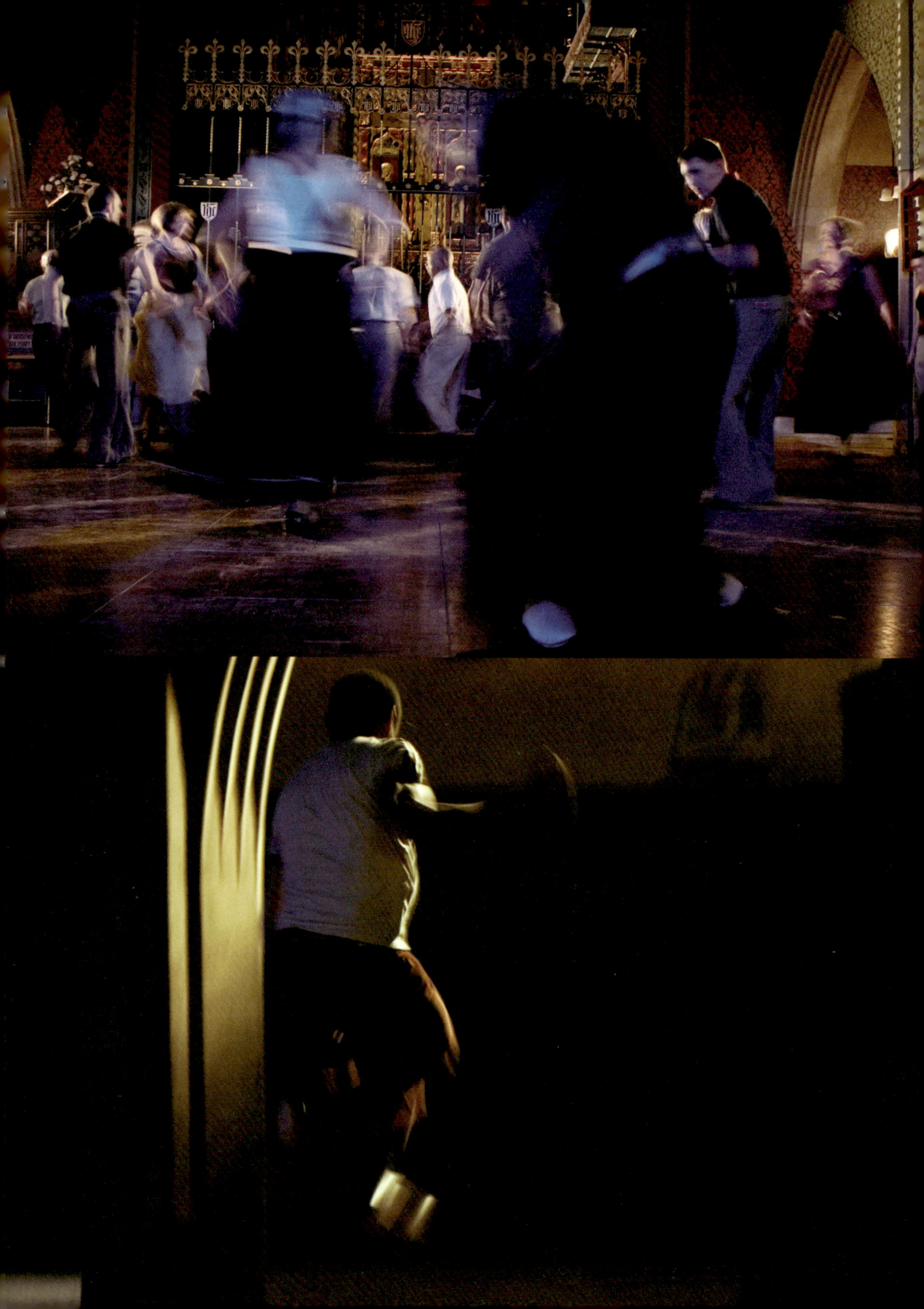

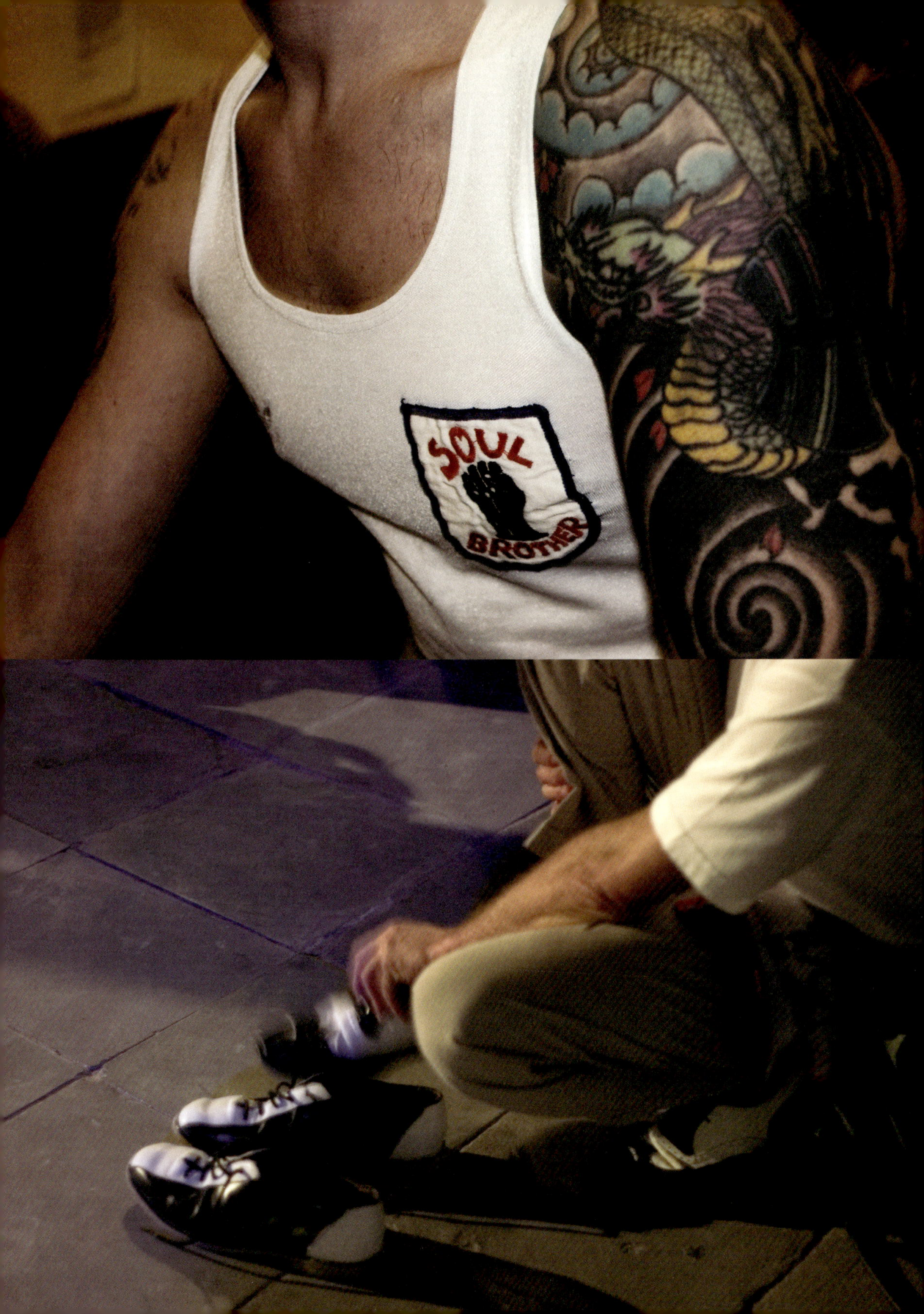
SOUL
BROTHER

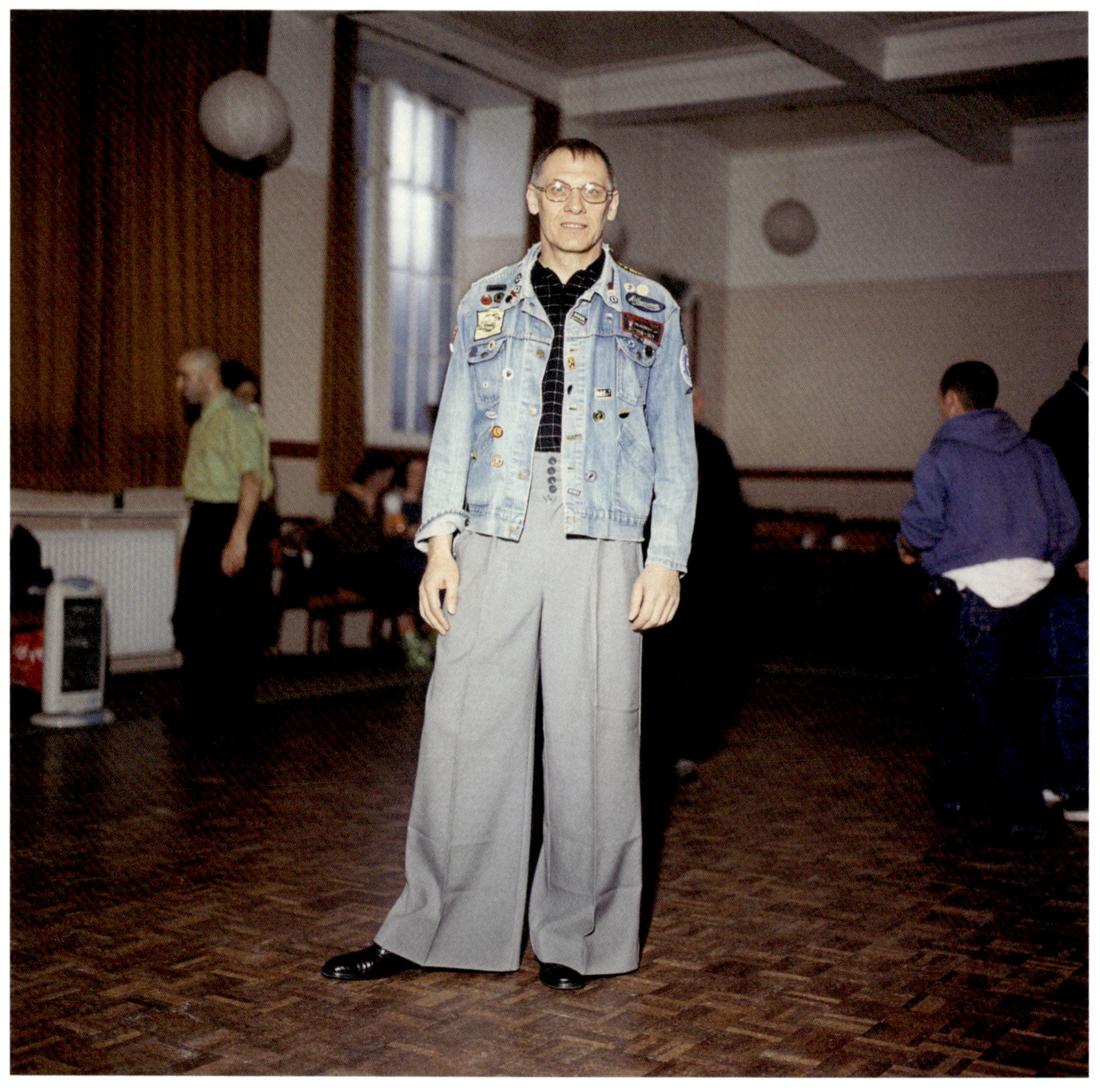

Terry

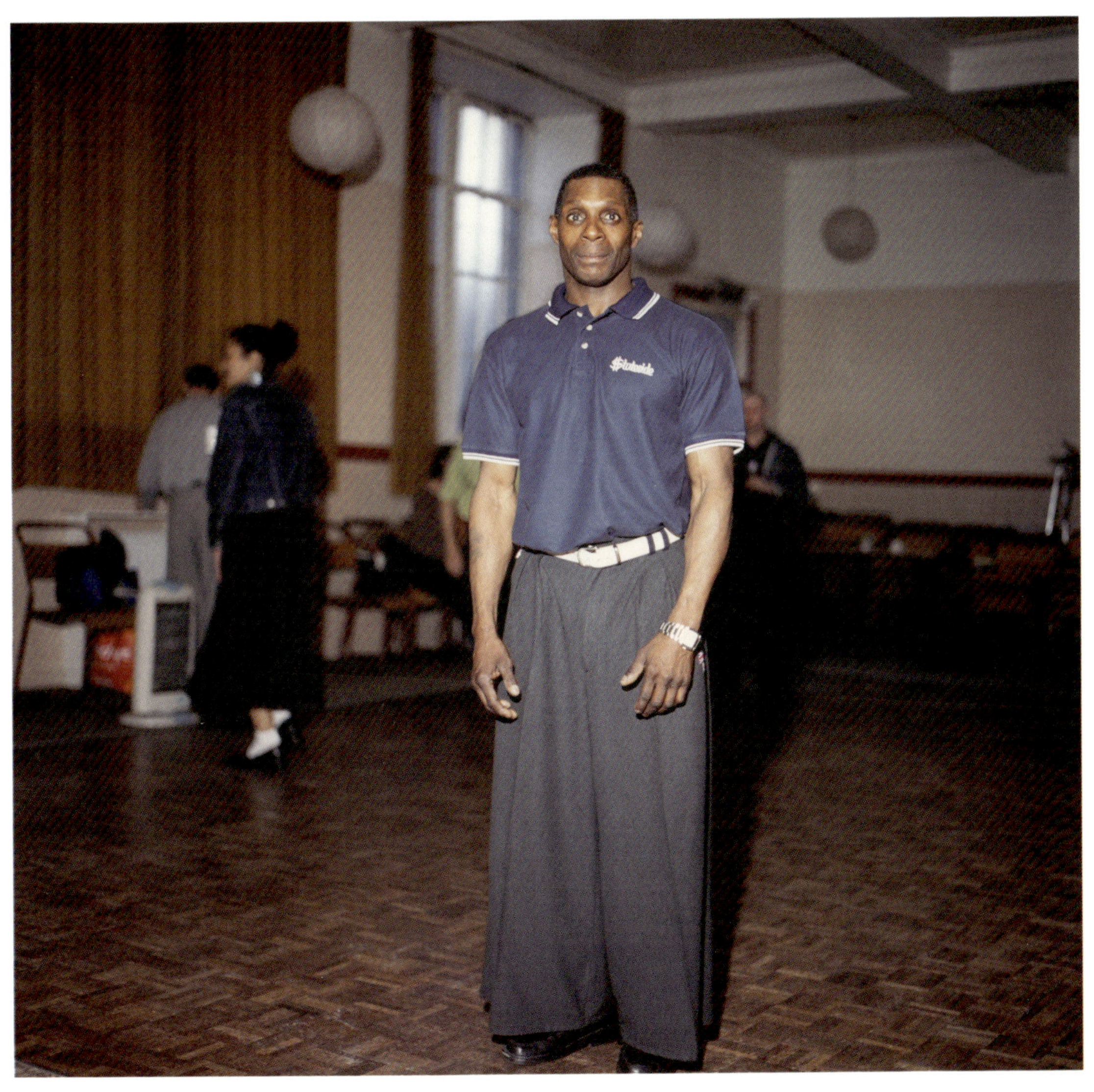

Carl

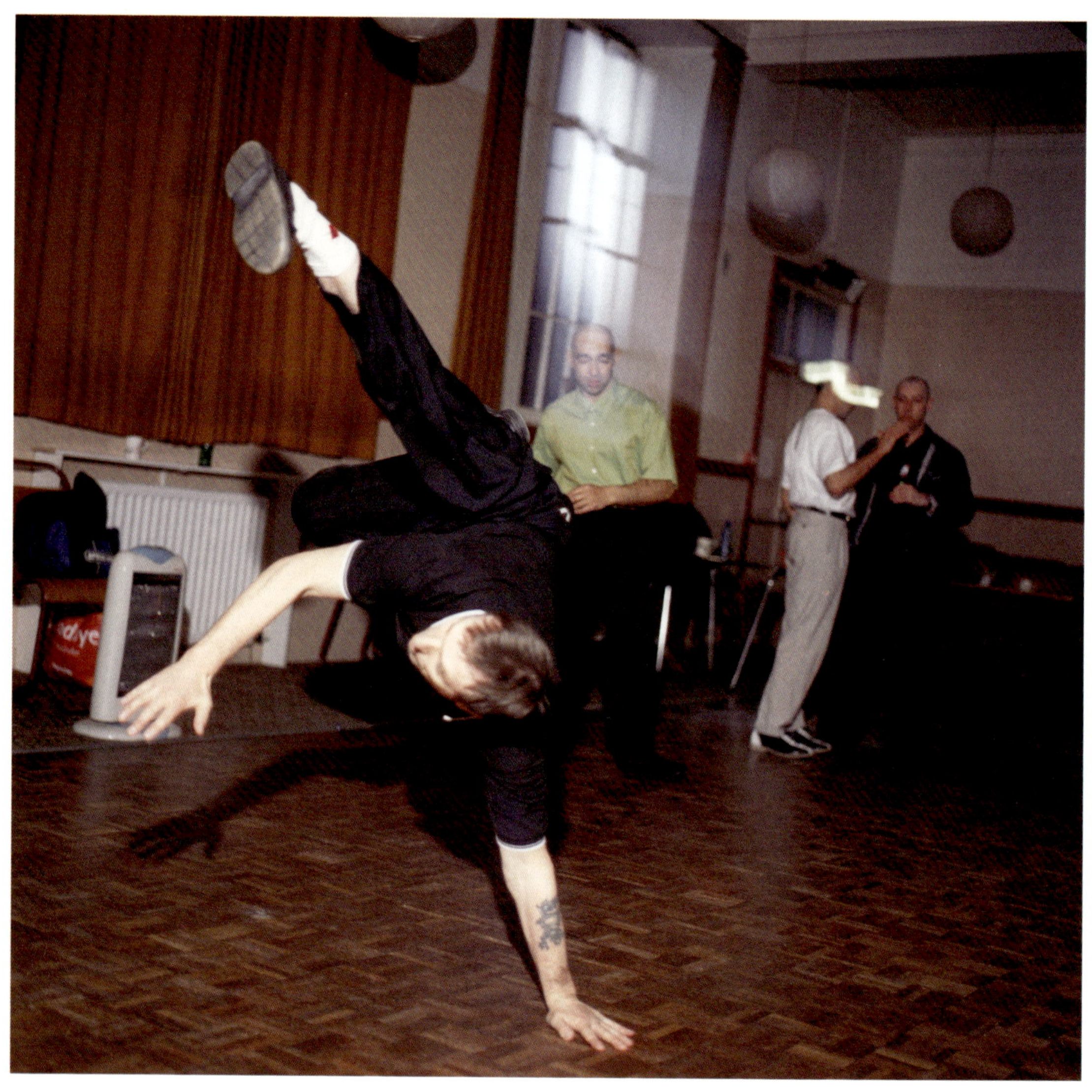

Andy

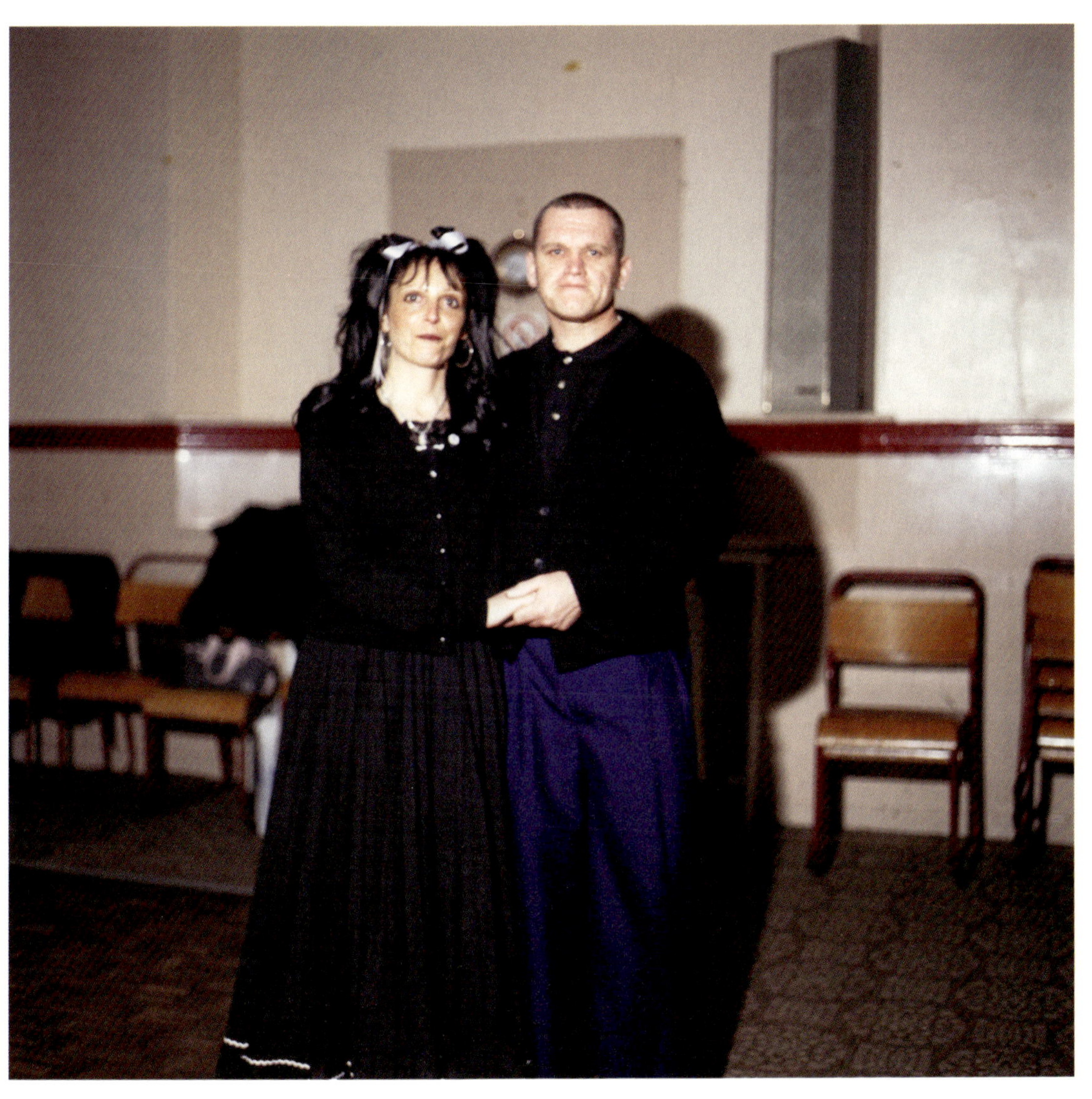

Judy and Colin

Keepin' the Faith

Rob Tufnell

Matt Stokes' film **Long After Tonight** (2005) opens to a crepuscular view of a Dundee street. Inside a church, a group of middle-aged men and women are recorded dancing in a dimly lit nave overlooked by austere carved and gilded effigies of a crucified Jesus, Mary, his mother and St John the Baptist. The real-time and slowed footage is accompanied by instrumental versions of the Northern Soul tracks 'The World Again' and 'Sidras Theme'. The dancers are dressed in associated fashions of the 1970s: Oxford bags, cotton singlets, long, pleated skirts and American style, two-toned, ten-pin bowling shirts. They skip and appear to glide across the polished parquet floor entirely self-involved as if each is in receipt of some spiritual charismata. Others, apparently consumed by some form of prevenient grace, engage in proto-break-dancing. The motley assembly resembles a group of religious heretics – Shakers, Quakers or Girlingites. The film concludes where it began, and loops – once again we glimpse Dundee's dawn and/or dusk simultaneously.

Long After Tonight documents the coming together of two churches, one Scottish Episcopalian, the other, a broader, secular church – the celebrants of Northern Soul. The former are represented by the architectural setting: St Salvador's Church in Dundee – one of the more significant 19th century Gothic Revival ecclesiastical interiors, designed by George Frederick Bodley.[1] The latter, fill the church with sound and movement. Both churches could be described as having declining and ageing congregations but would otherwise appear unrelated.[2]

Superficially Stokes' film follows a long-tested artistic strategy that probably began with drug-fuelled, shamanic fantasies of mythical creatures – half-man, half-beast – mermaids and minotaurs. A strategy that again became popular among artists during the first half of the last century in the aftermath of the First World War and with the work Sigmund Freud had pioneered into the subconscious. Stokes, like other contemporary artists working in a phenomenological tradition, is similarly interested in how things that appear opposite are essentially the same.

---

1   Prior to the Reformation, church congregations were expected to participate passively – to listen to sermons and look at paintings and effigies. The Reformation stressed The Word, and interpretations, pictorial, sculptural or performed were considered a distraction. The High Church or Kirk – whose beliefs were manifested in the Gothic revivalism of the 19th century as seen in the works of George Frederick Bodley, and others – rejected this.

2   During the early 1970s, the community halls attached to St Salvador's Church were used for Dundee's first Northern Soul sessions, and became fondly known by many as 'Sally's'.

Northern Soul, although less than 40 years old, can seem as
Baroque in its development as 2000 years of Christian theology. Northern
Soul is, simply put, African American Soul music from the 1960s
transferred to northern Britain. Unaltered, it was its dislocation from its
original context and era that prompted the establishment of a distinct
genre. The term was coined by David Godin who in 1968 established Soul
City, the first record shop in Britain dedicated to black music. Soul music
had become popular with British Mods in the 1960s who would dance
to sanitised African American Pop under the influence of Amphetamine
Sulphate. The introduction of Funk in about 1967 caused a subtle schism.
In the more intimate clubs of southern Britain the shift from two-four to
one-three was embraced – whilst in the larger dance halls and workers'
clubs in the North audiences kept faith with the conventional tempo.
Eager to feel progressive, the search for more musical material continued
as DJs resurrected increasingly obscure and esoteric Soul recordings
from the past. It was Godin who first identified this shift based upon
what records people sought in his shop. Around 1970, he established a
section in his store for 'Northern Soul' – dedicated to the tastes of his
customers from the north of England and Scotland – and also introduced
the term to his column in *Blues & Soul* magazine.

At this point Soul music was itself only ten years old. It had grown
out of the evangelical tradition and all its leading figures had come from
Gospel-singing backgrounds. The first such artist, following in the wake
of Ray Charles (who is credited with introducing 'spirit' to Rock and Roll),
was Sam Cooke. Famed as a church singer, Cooke had 'crossed over' from
Gospel to Pop in 1957 with considerable reticence as it meant 'serving
two masters'. Cooke's first such recording, 'Lovable', was released under
the pseudonym Dale Cook and sold 25,000 copies but led to a whispering
campaign by some of the 'faithful' who began to ostracise him. The
decision to make the permanent switch was thus forced upon him and his
first record release as Sam Cooke, 'You Send Me', reached the top of the
industry sales charts.[3]

The notion that secular music was necessarily profane has a long
tradition. The English Puritan, Jeremy Collier, in his *A Short View of
the Immorality and Profaneness of the Stage* (1699) for example, stated
that, 'Music is almost as dangerous as gunpowder, and it maybe requires
looking after no less than the press or the Mint.'[4] The Reverend Rowland
Hill, preacher and founder of Surrey Chapel on London's Blackfriars
Road, declared in the 1780s the often misquoted: 'the Devil should

---

3   Guralnick, Peter, *Sweet Soul Music, Rhythm and Blues and the Southern Dream of Freedom*, Canongate
Books, 2002
4   Hill, Christopher, *The World Turned Upside Down; Radical Ideas During the English Revolution*, p385, Pelican
Books, 1975

not have all the best tunes.' In the African American tradition, there is also the legend that Robert Johnson, and others, sold their souls to the Devil in return for musical prowess.[5] Those immersed in Gospel would not have been surprised at Cooke's death in 1964 (from a gunshot wound outside a three-dollar-a-night Los Angeles motel inappropriately named the Hacienda). In 1960, when Solomon Burke (who led his own church – Solomon's Temple: The House of God for All People) was signed to Atlantic records, he was reluctant to be associated with irreligious music. Objecting to being marketed as a Rhythm and Blues singer, Burke consulted his congregation before settling on *Soul* – a term proposed by Jerry Wexler (then Vice President of Atlantic records).[6]

It was long assumed that the roots of African American music were to be found on the African continent, brought to the Americas by slaves. However, recent research by Willie Ruff, a Professor of music at Yale University suggests otherwise. Ruff remembered an anecdote from jazz trumpeter Dizzy Gillespie that the origins of black American church music lay in the Outer Hebrides of Scotland, not Africa. Gillespie claimed that his grandparents had told him how in North and South Carolina slave masters took their workers to church with them where they spoke and worshipped in Gaelic.[7]

Ruff claims however that there are still descendants of African slaves in Kentucky, 'Old Regular Baptists', who 'cling to the formative elements of the "old way" of congregational singing.'[8] And in Alabama he has noted a small congregation of black Presbyterians 'holding onto the line, singing what white Presbyterians in America and in other parts of the English-speaking world abandoned more than a century ago.'[9] He continues: 'It makes sense that as we got our names from the slave masters, we carried the slave owners blood, their religion and their customs, that we should have adopted and adapted their music. There are more descendants of Highland Scots living in America than there are in the Highlands – and a great many of them are black... I have been to Africa many times in search of my cultural identity, but it was in the Highlands that I found the cultural roots of black America.'[10]

An ongoing series of performances **Sacred Selections** (2005–) organised by Stokes in civic halls and churches in Dundee, London,

---

5   Johnson's song 'Cross Road Blues' is said to describe the transaction at the junction of US Highways 61 and 49 in Clarksdale, Mississippi.

6   Guralnick, Peter, *op cit*

7   http://www.willieruff.com/linesinging.html

8   The first book published in America is said to have been the Boston Bay Psalm Book in 1640. This was a user-friendly collection of metrical Psalms, intended to assist in congregational 'line singing'. After the Protestant Reformation congregations were not only permitted but also encouraged to participate actively in worship. Amongst largely illiterate, impoverished peoples 'precenting the line' was an obvious means.

9   http://www.willieruff.com/linesinging.html

10   *ibid*

Norwich, Edinburgh, Rotterdam and Dublin, operates across similar
traditions and tensions – some profound, others trivial. **Sacred Selections**
has seen anthems of Northern Soul, Happy Hardcore and Black Metal
transcribed for, and performed on, pipe organs. Two venues that
have hosted the project, St Laurens' Church, Rotterdam and St Giles'
Cathedral, Edinburgh, rather than being calm and reserved sanctuaries
are re-evaluated by Stokes.

St Laurens', completed in 1525, (dedicated to the patron saint of
Rotterdam and sometime acting Bishop of Rome who 'trod the furious
pagan world underfoot and flung aside its allurements, [thus gaining]
victory over Satan's attack on his faith'[11]) was one of only three prominent
buildings in the city to survive bombing in 1940. It was also once host
to a 17th century library of the works of Desiderius Erasmus whose
translation of the New Testament into Greek and satirical writings
addressing Church corruption proved to be catalysts of the Reformation.

St Giles' Cathedral (not actually a cathedral but nonetheless the
religious focal point within Scotland's capital for 900 years) is the mother
church of Presbyterianism. It is also where the English Civil War is said
to have begun in 1637 when Charles I attempted to impose Anglican
services upon the Scottish Church with the Book of Common Prayer.
Like most British churches, St Giles', is filled with celebrations of violence
in the form of military banners, war memorials and chapels dedicated to
knights.

The performances of Black Metal on church organs might appear
to be particularly jarring given the genre's close association with
church arson. Kristian Vikernes, a leading figure in the Black Metal
movement, is currently serving a 22-year sentence for the murder of a
colleague and for the burning of three churches in Bergen, Vindafjord
and Oslo. Vikernes is also believed to have been responsible for the
destruction of Fantoft Stavkirke in Bergen (a church dating from 1150).
His justification for the arson was that the churches he burnt were
themselves desecrations having been built upon pre-Christian, pagan
sites of significance.

Sacred Selections, with the potential to offend one or other of the
contradictory cultures that are generated by differing belief systems,
reminds us that for some a revision will always be a blasphemy – be it
when songs are rearranged, texts are translated or buildings extended
or refitted. It would, however, be a mistake to miss the humour in Matt
Stokes' work. Within this there is satire, but then more simply, the idea
that things that appear to be in the wrong place are funny. As a friend of

---

11   *Old Sarum Rite Missal*, from the Mass for the Octave (Apodosis) of Saint Laurence, 17 August 1525, Saint
Hilarion Press, 1998

mine pointed out there is a comic precedent to Stokes' activity, albeit in a wholly different context. Episode 132 of the Simpsons, 'Bart Sells His Soul'[12] sees Bart serving as a church usher. He switches the organist's intended sheet music with something labelled 'In the Garden of Eden' by I. Ron Butterfly (a thinly veiled 'In-A-Gadda-Da-Vida' – Iron Butterfly's legendary psychedelic rock anthem[13]). Milhouse, having fingered Bart to the Reverend Lovejoy, explains to Bart that he feared crows pecking at his soul for eternity if he didn't tell. Bart scoffs at the very notion of having a soul, saying there is no such thing: 'Soul? Come on, Milhouse, there is no such thing as a soul. It's just something they made up to scare kids, like the boogeyman or Michael Jackson.'

Stokes' most recent film **Cipher** (2006), follows **Sacred Selections** and **Long After Tonight** but is instead set in a secular setting. The film records two organists performing within Edinburgh's Usher Hall. The score, created for the film, transfers something of the sounds of Fimbulvetr, a 'dark Ambient musick club' (*sic*), from the amplifiers of Pleasance's Cabaret Bar to the pipe organ of the city's largest music venue.[14] Composed by pipe organists Kevin Bowyer and John Riley (working together with the club promoters, Dan Hunt and Neil Howie) the composition sees discordance and drone applied to classical organ structures (inspired by the 'ambient' and 'extreme' sounds played at Fimbulvetr, and the apocalyptic mythologies connected to the origins of the club's name).

The Usher Hall resulted from a bequest to the city in 1896 by whisky distiller, Andrew Usher for the construction of a concert venue. The hall provides a home for the Royal Scottish National Orchestra but has also hosted rock concerts, boxing matches and in 1972, the Eurovision Song Contest. It was also famed for political assemblies. In 1914 Prime Minister Herbert Asquith gave a speech there calling for volunteers to enlist, and in the 1930s concerts were held to raise money for the Spanish Republicans. A riot on the Lothian Road in 1934 following an address by British Fascist leader Sir Oswald Mosely closed the hall to political events. Something of this camp and chaotic history is explored in **Cipher**.

In the film's opening sequence, the camera moves from the hall, flooded with appropriately cold light, to the basement where the pump

---

12   First broadcast on 8 October 1995. Directed by Wesley Archer and written by Greg Daniels.

13   'In-A-Gadda-Da-Vida' itself, like Stokes' activity, involves something of a mistranslation. Released in 1968, this 17-minute track (released on an album sharing the same title) was, according to legend, originally titled 'In the Garden of Eden' but singer Doug Ingle, under the influence of LSD, slurred the words when drummer Ron Bushy asked him the title.

14   In Norse mythology Fimbulvetr is the immediate prelude to Ragnarok – the end of the world. It was believed to consist of three successive winters without any intervening summer. During such a time, there would be constant warfare. In Old Norse, the word translates as 'The Great Winter'.

engine turns over, then back to the hall and the pipe loft flanked by two trumpet wielding cherubim. In turn, the two earnest-looking organists pummel the console with their hands, feet and forearms. The film ends with the camera finding its focus looking up at the pipes. Silent, they appear to breathe. The Usher Hall takes on a menace that brings to mind the home of Edgar Allan Poe's Roderick Usher rather than Andrew Usher's Hall.[15]

Stokes' film dissects the hall's pipe organ as if it were an anatomical organ – from the blower room in the bowels of the building to the extensive array of pipes, at its heart. As an organism it is somewhat discombobulated – its intake and output being at the wrong ends. We see the various toe and thumb pistons, and draw stops with their Gnostic labelling. One such stop bears the legend *voix céleste* – but the *heavenly voice* of the pipe organ is deliberately off pitch. Regardless of what the Reverend Rowland Hill might have hoped, organ builders know that the Devil does have all the best tunes.

Real Arcadia, another ongoing work, initiated in 2003, applies a similar methodology to Acid House. Often linked to Northern Soul, Acid House has an equally complex mythology. Like Northern Soul it was adopted and adapted in Britain from America but rather than appropriating anaemic, black Pop music, Acid House embraced the harder, mid-eighties sounds of the African American and gay club scenes of Chicago and New York (via the nightclubs of the Balearic islands of the Western Mediterranean). Similarly, Acid House was driven by its music, associated fashions and the influence of prohibited drugs, and found a new and wider relevance once it crossed the Atlantic. However, unlike Northern Soul, its rapid shift to mainstream appeal prompted Government legislation as, for a very brief moment in 1989, it did appear (at least to the tabloid press) as genuinely revolutionary. Accordingly Acid House 'parties' came to carry a legal definition: 'a gathering... of 100 or more persons... at which amplified music is played during the night (with or without intermissions)... "music" includes sounds wholly or predominantly characterised by the emission of a succession of repetitive beats.'[16]

Stokes' exploration of the genre was initiated during a period of residency in Grizedale Forest, the Forestry Commission's sculpture park overlooking Coniston Water in Cumbria. Here, in the landscape that inspired the English Romantic movement, his enquiry became speleological as it addressed a scene that however popular, was literally

---

15   Roderick Usher, the fictional protagonist of Poe's short story *The Fall of the House of Usher* (1839), believed his home to be haunted.

16   From the Criminal Justice and Public Order Act 1994, 'Powers in relation to raves': chapters 63-66.

underground. In the Lake District raves were not only held in clubs, warehouses or fields, as elsewhere, but also within a cave system in the side of a mountain called Holm Fell.

In its present state, **Real Arcadia** takes the form of a museological display. Vitrines are filled with the fading ephemera of Outhouse Promotions – the organisers of these events in the early 1990s. We are presented with cassette tapes complied by the troglodyte sounding DJs Grog, Powie, Slebby and Steely. Photocopied flyers, misshapen t-shirts and snapshots. A speaker stack meticulously reproduced by Stokes from photographs and contemporary accounts of Outhouse's battered, amateur sound system. There is also a video of computer generated mapping of the cave and local news footage – where it is suggested that Lord Egremont, the landowner, was to dynamite the cave. Behind this Stokes displays banners with quotes taken from interviews with organisers and party-goers. The texts take on the significance (if not the craft) of a temperance or trade union gonfalon expounding fragments of the philosophy (such as it was). One concludes '… it was for the people. We never charged a penny.'

Like **Long After Tonight**, **Sacred Selections** and **Cipher**, **Real Arcadia** looks at incongruity and finds its opposite. If Stokes' archived accounts are to be believed then the parties overlooking Coniston were a Romantic response, totally befitting their context, to a scene very short on idealism by 1991 when the 'Rave in the Cave' nights took place (some two years after the wider Acid culture had peaked). Acid House had by then largely dissolved into a myriad of further subcultures quicker than it had formed into a single mainstream one. Those quick to exploit the scene had accelerated its demise – crap record producers and club promoters, kitsch design (found in fashions and flyers) and gun toting gangsters punting 'security', stolen sound systems and a ready source of MDMA, cut variously with domestic cleaning products, Paracetamol, LSD, Strychnine and, Northern Soul's drug of choice, the time-honoured, cheap teenage upper, Amphetamine Sulphate.

Real Arcadia exists in the muddy, Neo-Classical tradition most famously explored by Nicholas Poussin in his painting of shepherds of the Peloponnesian peninsula.[17] Arcadia has come to be understood as the definitive geographical Utopia although its harsh, arid mountain landscape is far from the lush environment the name may bring to mind. The landscape John Ruskin championed as an English Arcadia, and now thought by the local constabulary and landowners to be unsuitable for teenage parties, is the same landscape that so inspired 18th and 19th century hedonists Samuel Taylor Coleridge, Percy Bysshe Shelley,

---

17   'Les Bergers d'Arcadie', 1637-1638

Dorothy Wordsworth and their chronicler, the infamous opium eater, Thomas De Quincey who ingested Laudanum 'to an excess, not yet recorded of any other man.'[18] England's Arcadia, was never a quaint rural idyll as it may be understood today but something far grander, beautiful but terrible. In 1753, art collector Dr John Brown, described Keswick in the Lake District in terms of Romantic painting: 'The full perfection of Keswick consists of three circumstances, Beauty, Horror and Immensity united... But to give you a complete idea of these three perfections... would require the united powers of Claude [Lorrain], Salvator [Rosa], and Poussin. The first should throw his delicate sunshine over the cultivated vales. The second should dash out the horror of the rugged cliffs, the steeps, the hanging woods, and foaming waterfalls, while the grand pencil of Poussin should crown the whole with the majesty of the impending mountains.'[19]

Underpinning much of Matt Stokes' work is an exploration of the idea of 'religion'. Not of conventional, dogmatic faith systems but of collective worship in its most primitive sense – something looser, more celebratory, more profound if not more sensible – that began in caves at the naissance of civilisation – grounded more in the earth rather than the sky. Karl Marx's introduction to his *Critique of Hegel's Philosophy of Right* (1843) describes something of the territory Stokes explores: 'Religion is the general theory of this world, its encyclopedic compendium, its logic in popular form, its spiritual *point d'honneur*, its enthusiasm, its moral sanction, its solemn complement, and its universal basis of consolation and justification. It is the *fantastic realisation* of the human essence since the *human essence* has not acquired any true reality.'[20] With this in mind Stokes' works appear exegetical – exploring more recent examples of the *Opium des Volkes*[21] both literal and metaphorical – ingested both orally and aurally.

---

18   De Quincey, Thomas, *Confessions of an English Opium Eater*, p2, Oxford World's Classics, 2004

19   Quoted in Bicknell, P., *Beauty, Horror and Immensity: Picturesque Landscape in Britain 1750-1850*, pp1–2, Fitzwilliam Museum, Cambridge, 1981

20   Marx, Karl, *Critique of Hegel's Philosophy of Right* (1843), Cambridge University Press, 1970, (ed. Joseph O'Malley, translated by Annette Jolin and Joseph O'Malley)

21   Opiates held religious connotations long before Marx. In the 16th century Swiss chemist, Paracelsus named Laudanum (the opiate fashionable to the generation preceding Marx) after the Latin word *laudere* – to praise.

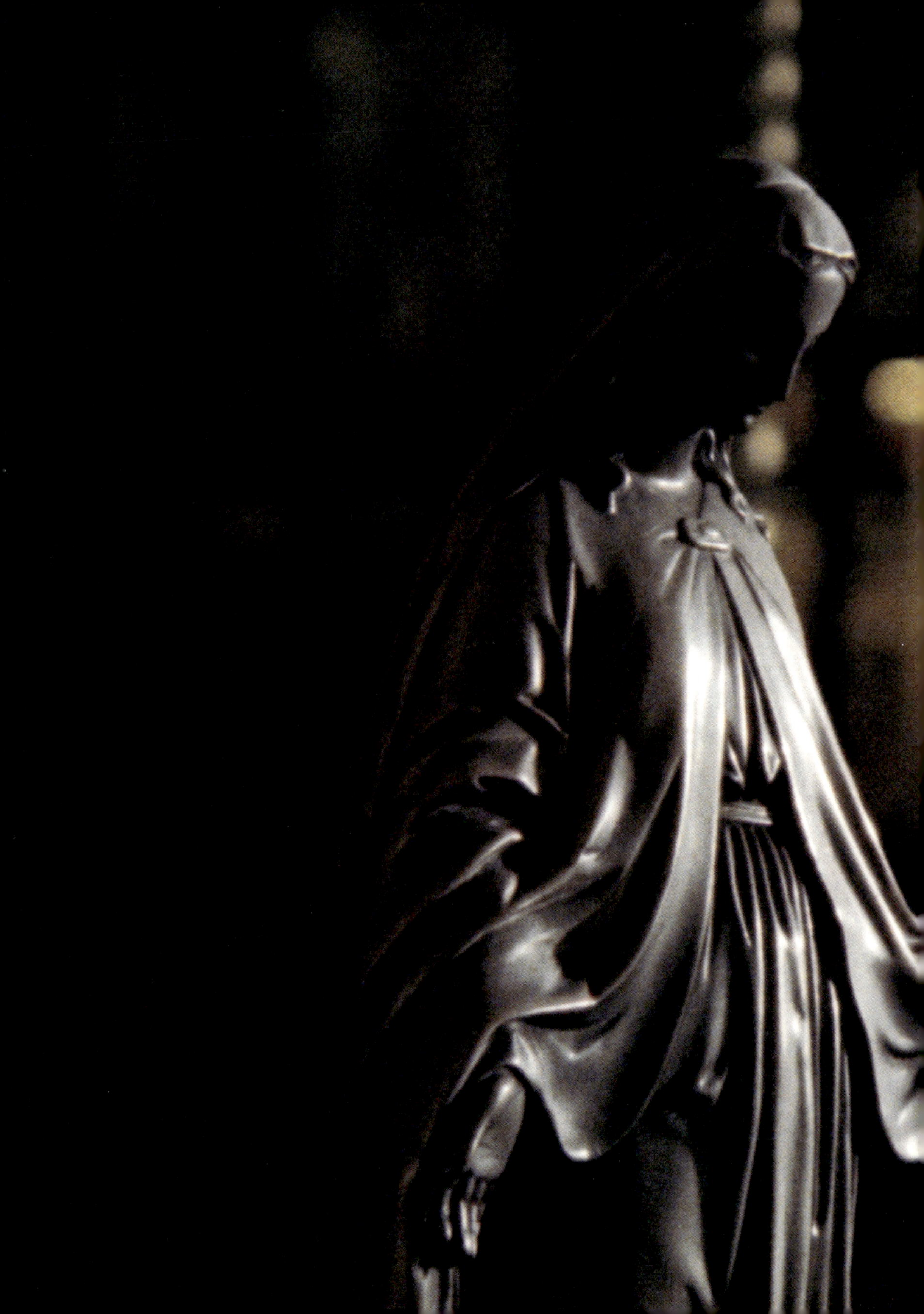

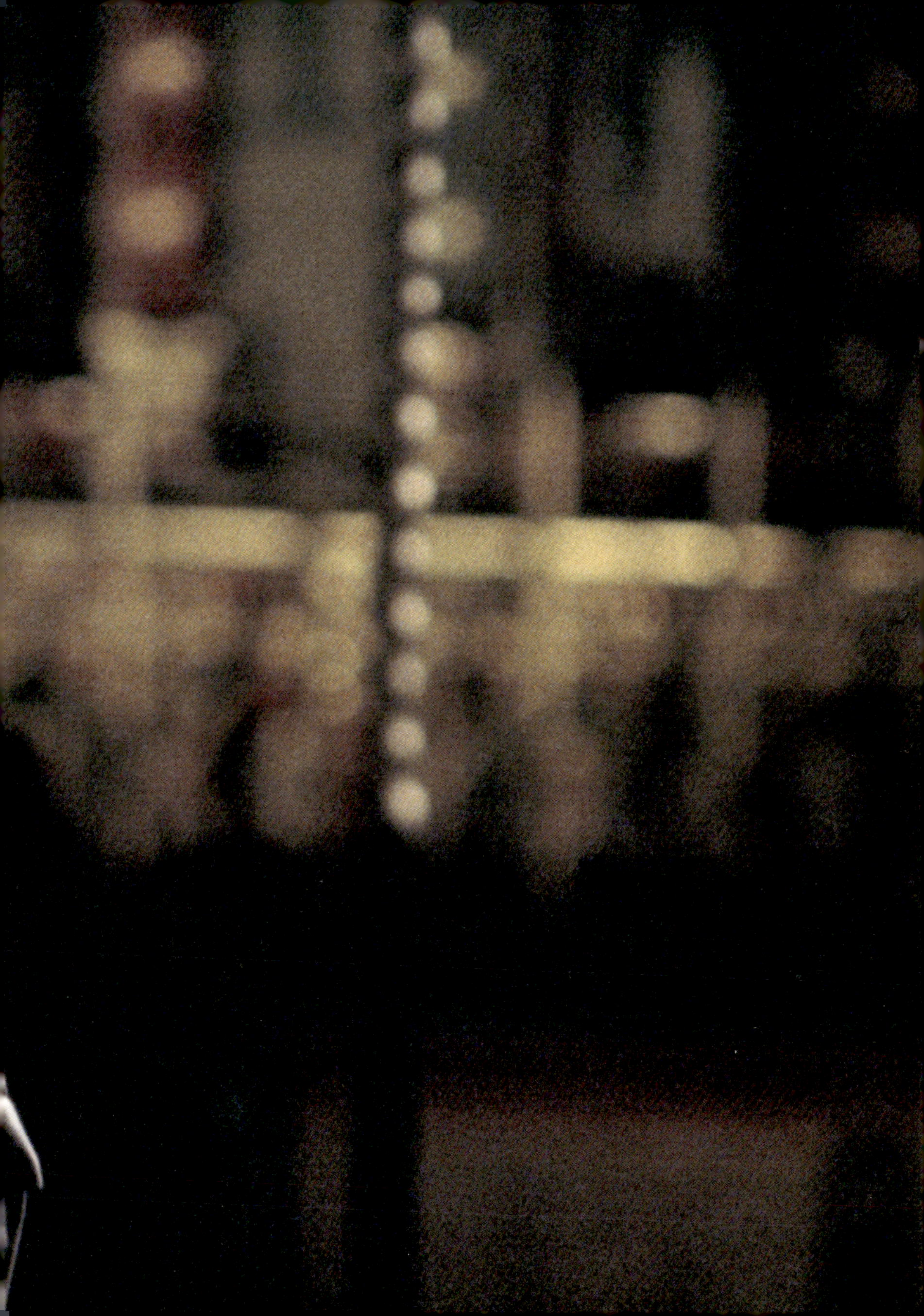

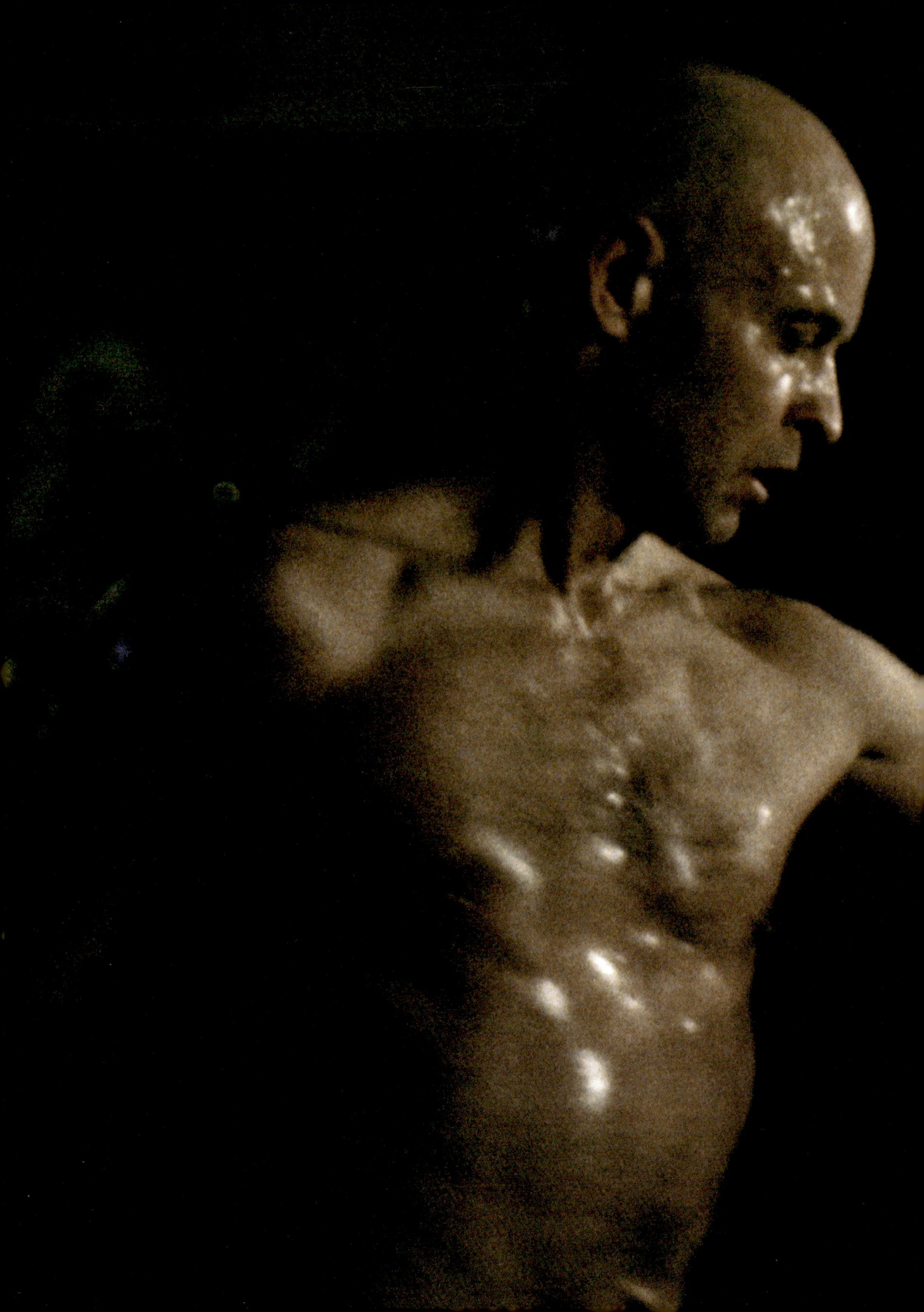

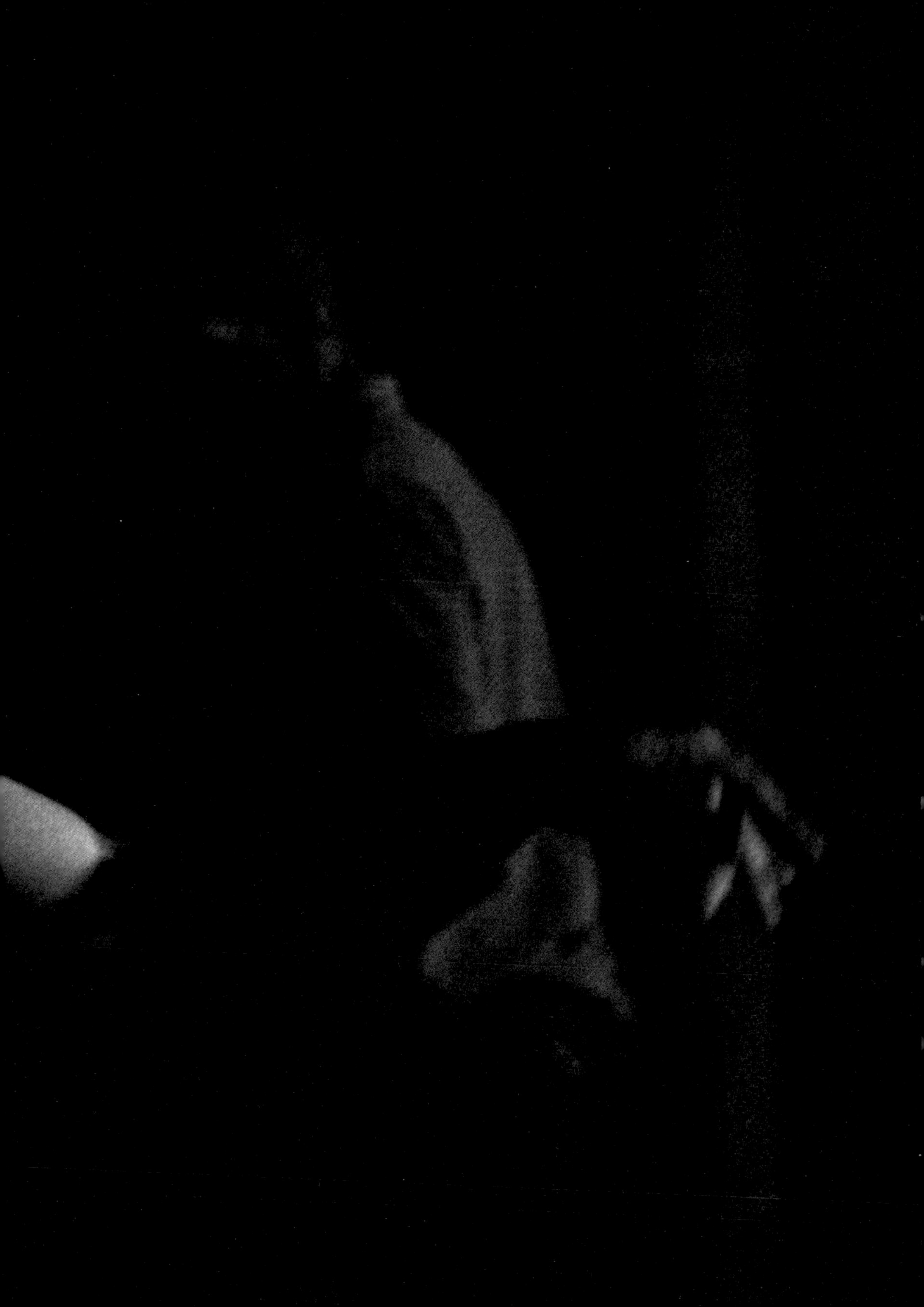

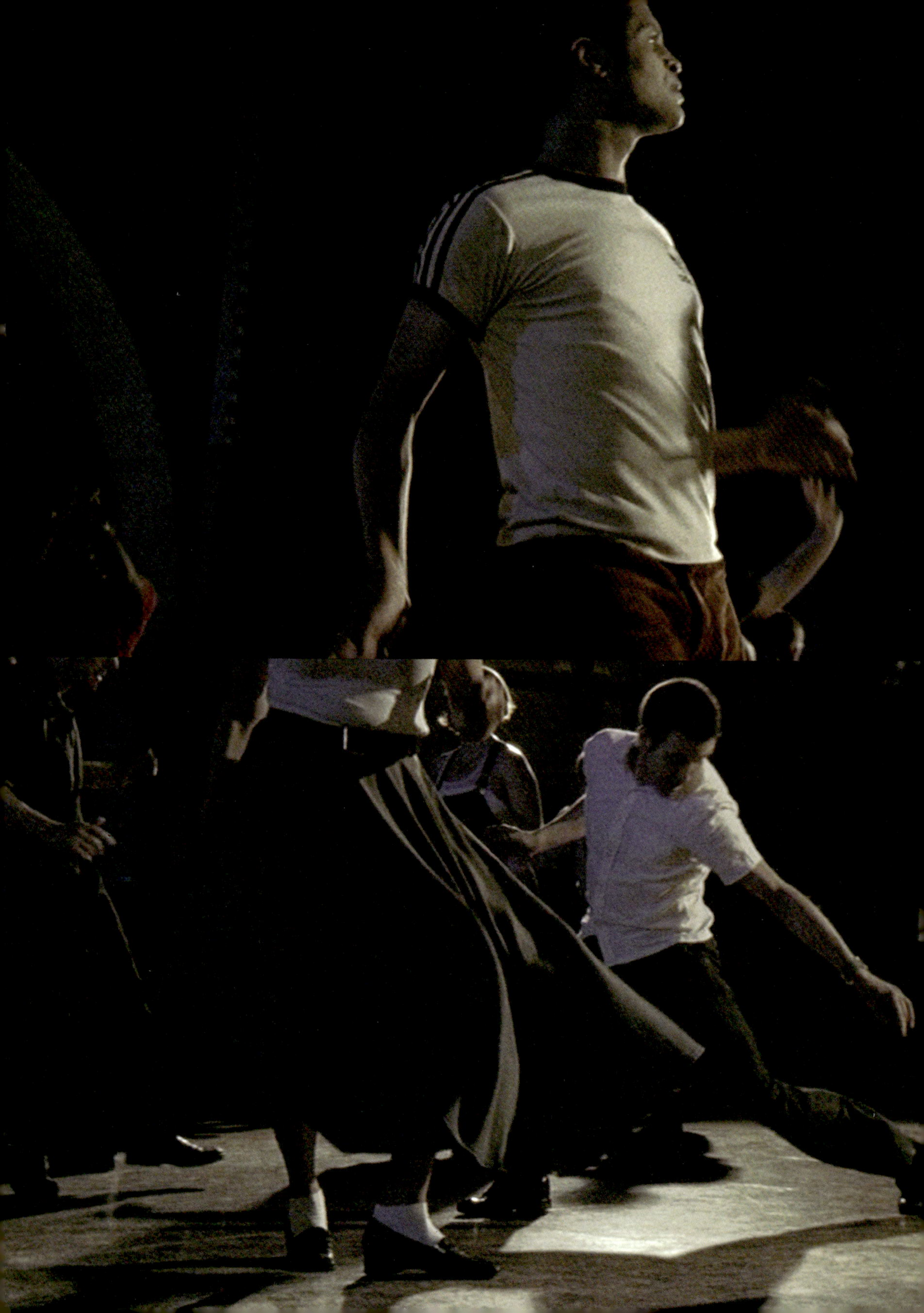

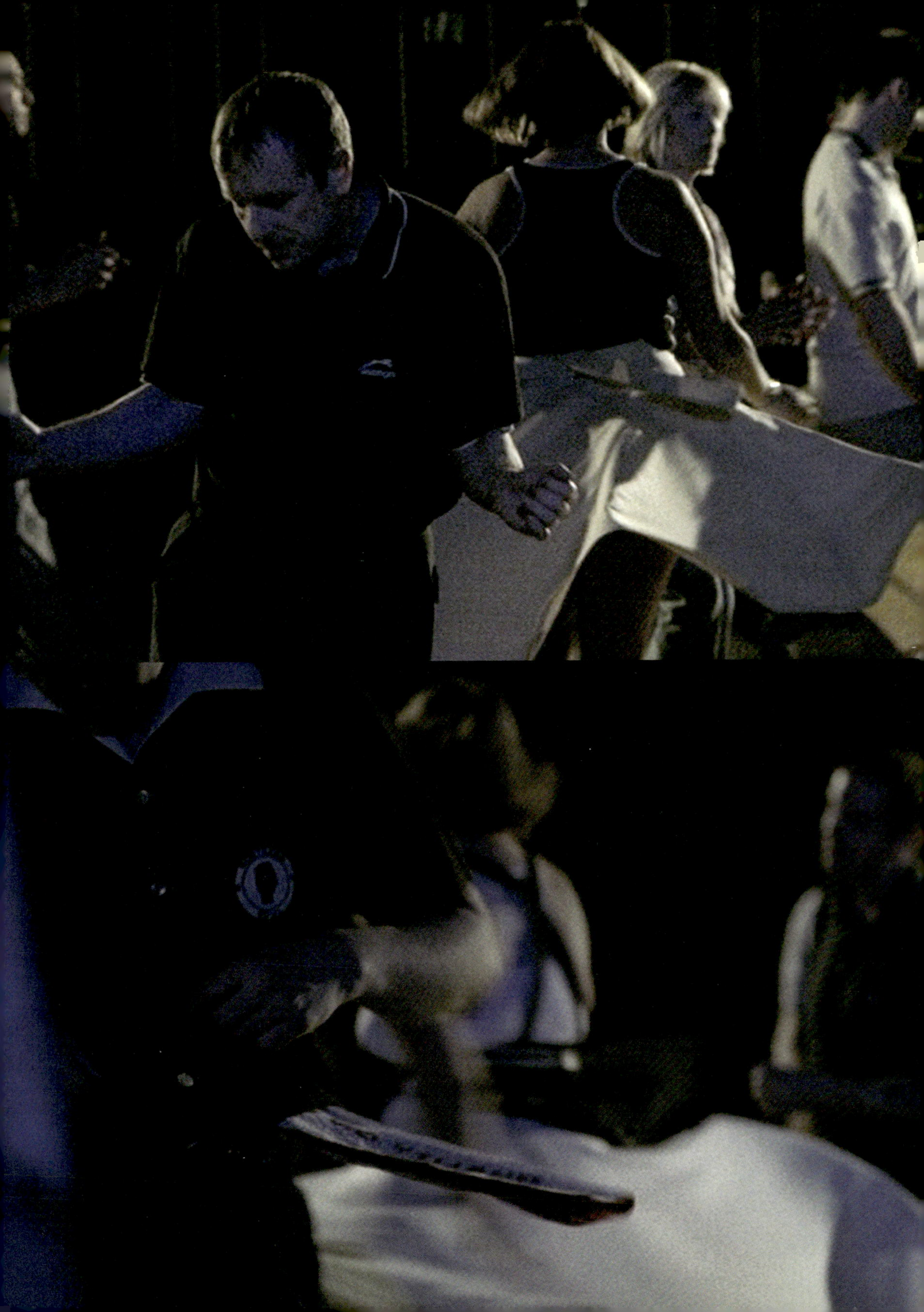

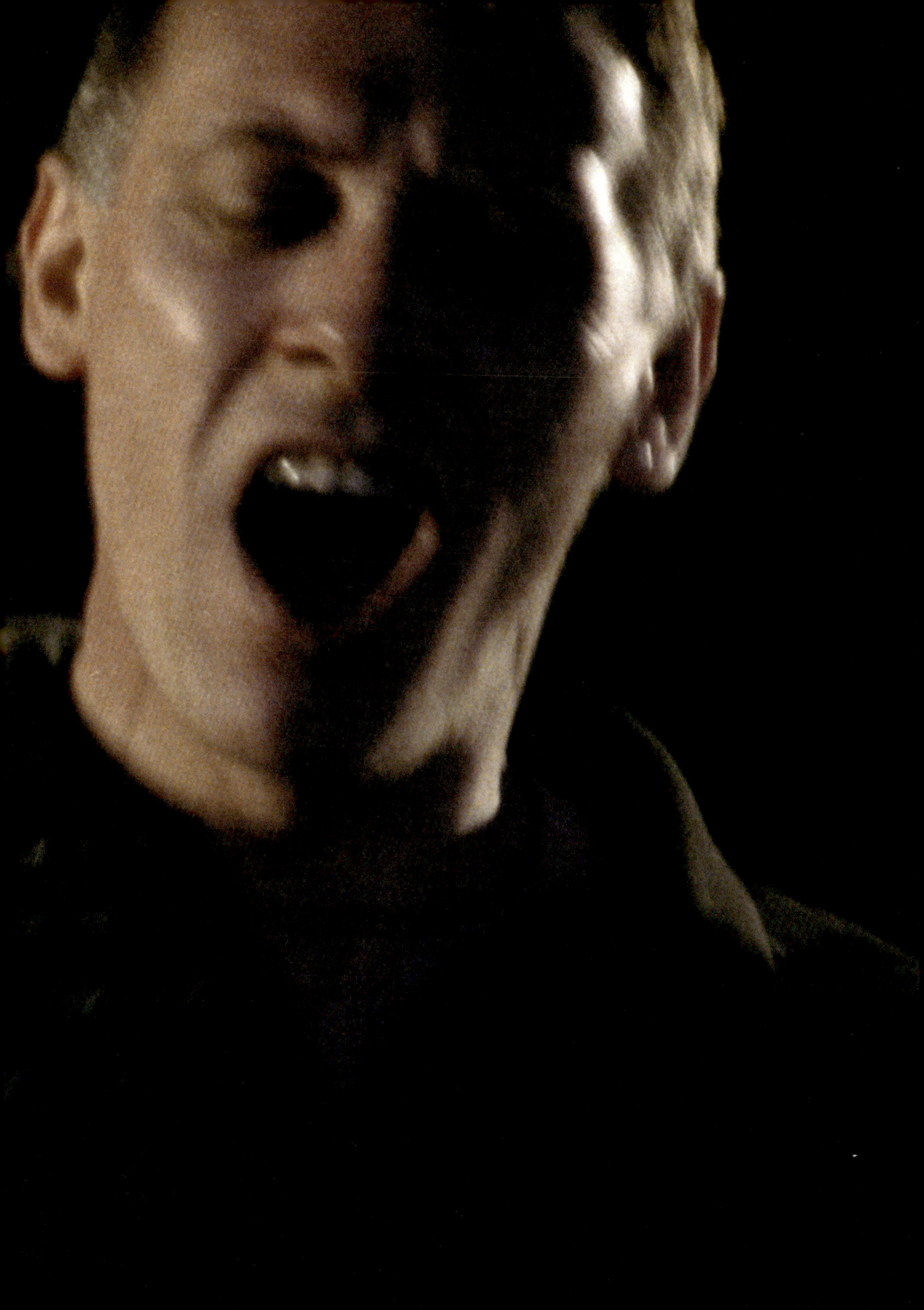

Cipher

Cipher
Super 16mm film and audio (transferred to DVD)
2006
Duration 9 minutes 56 seconds

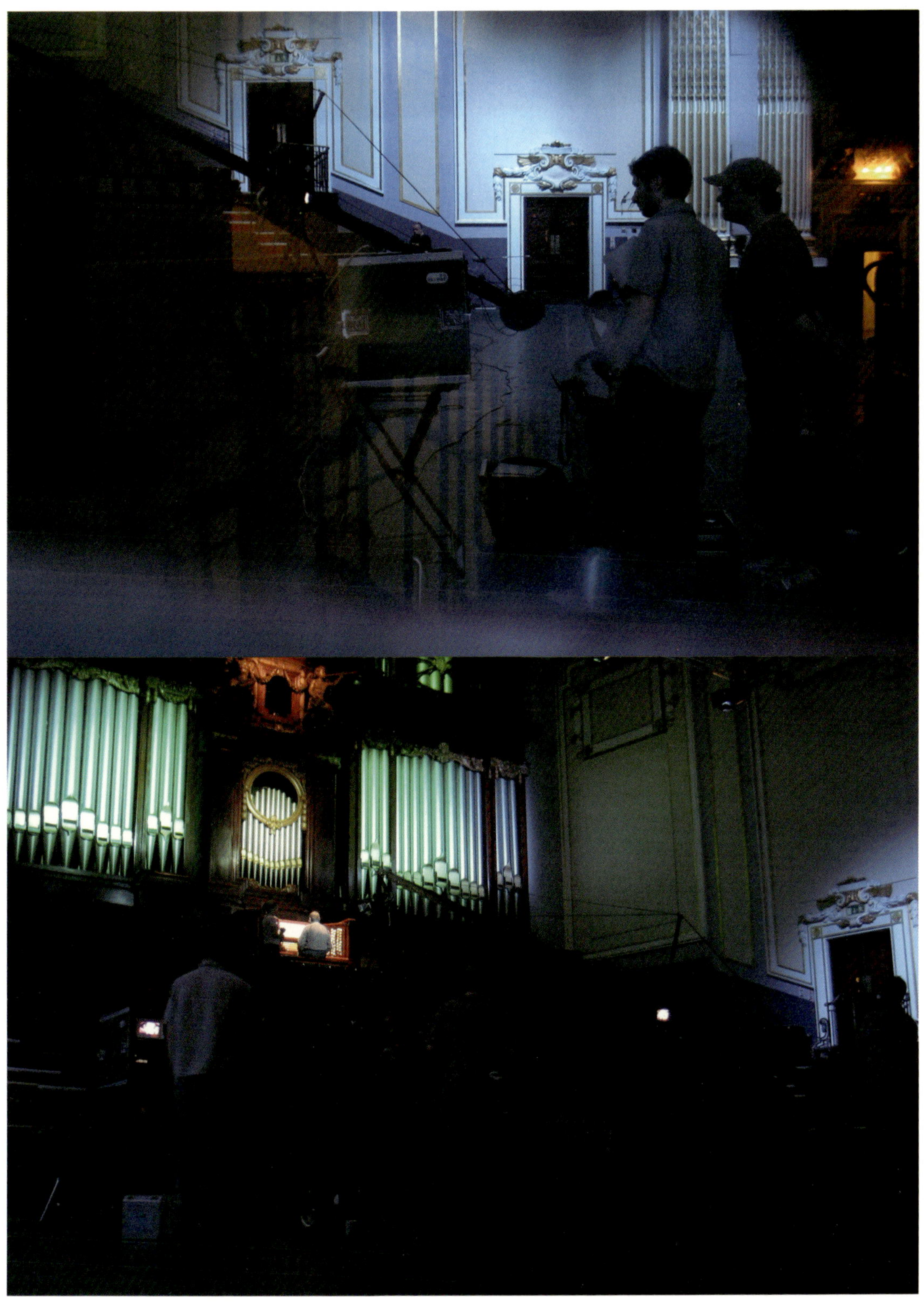

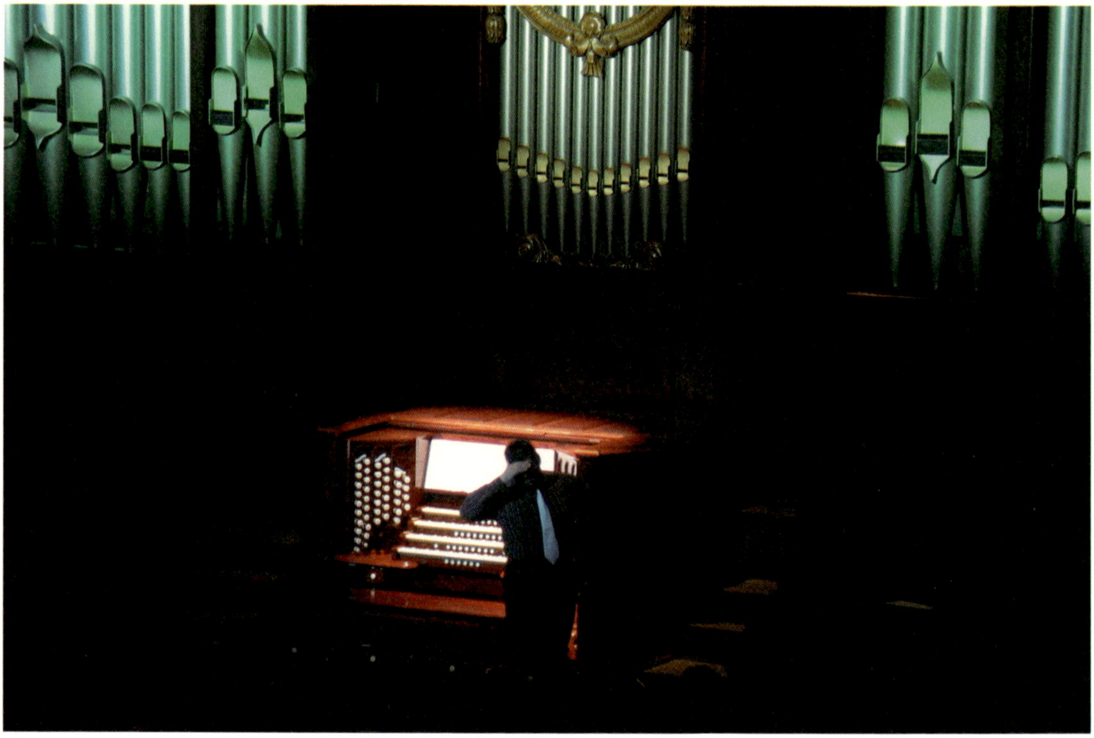

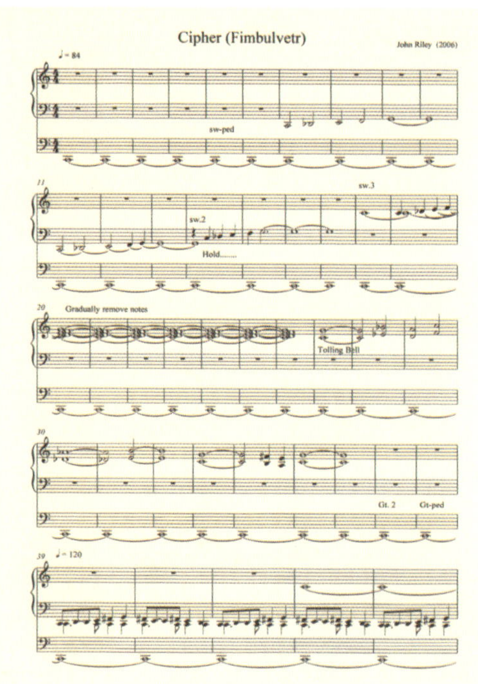
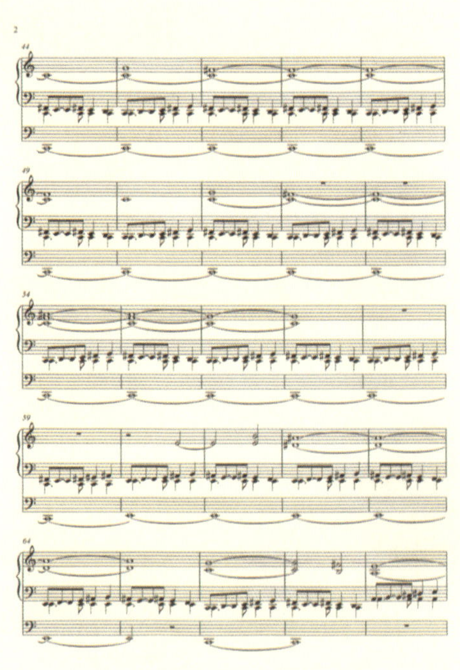

Pages from the score composed by John Riley for **Cipher**, in collaboration with Dan Hunt and Neil Howie.

34

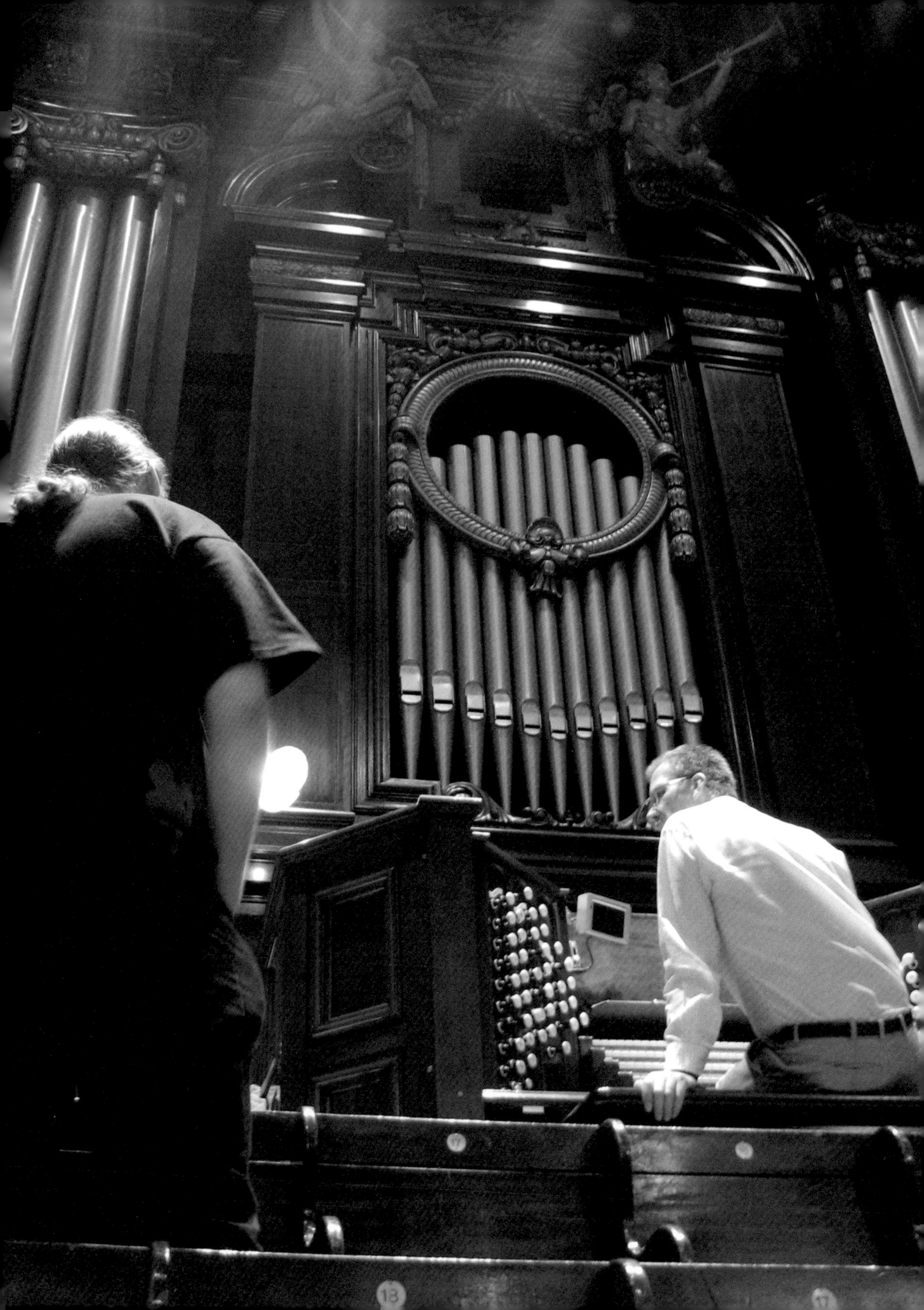

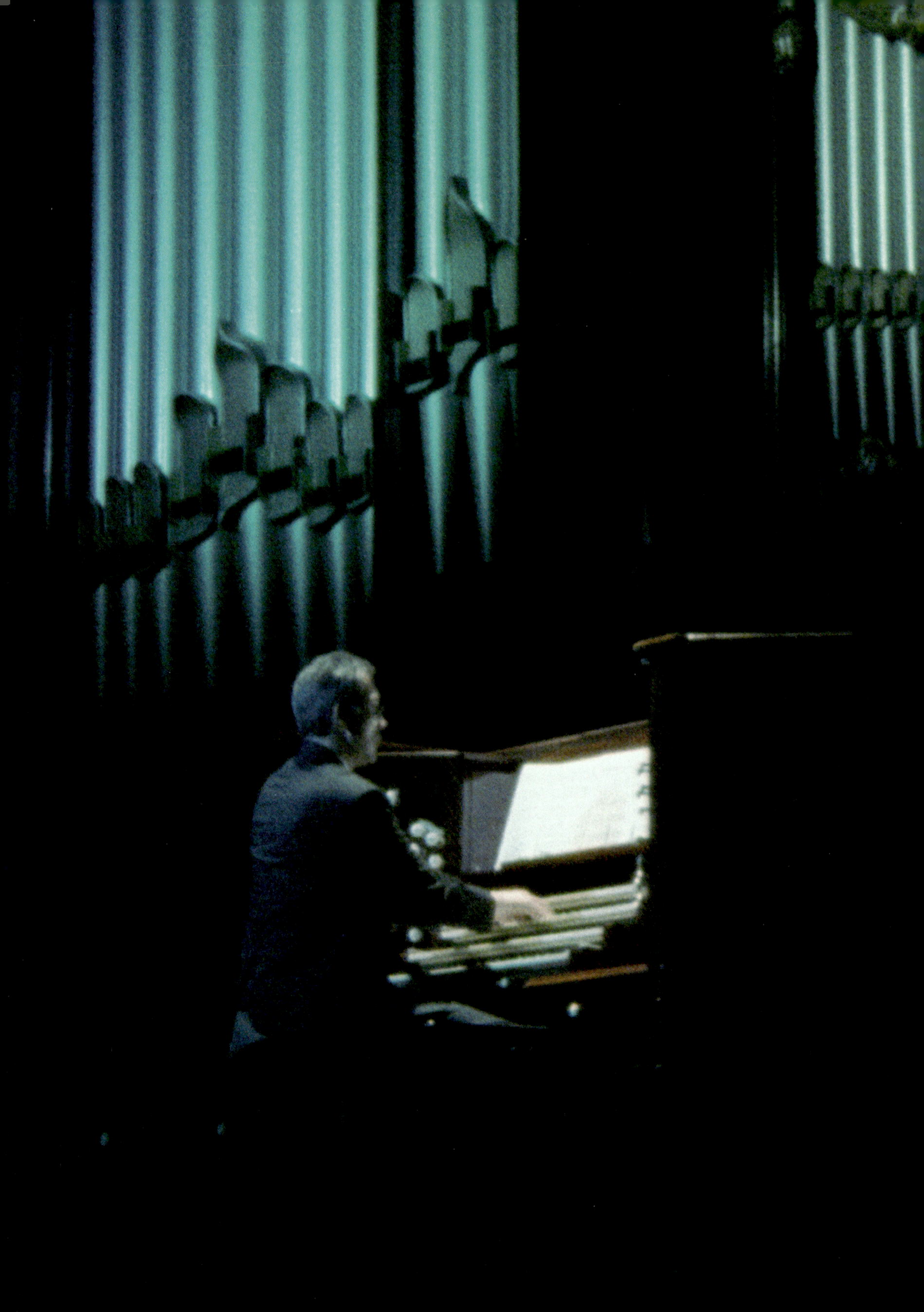

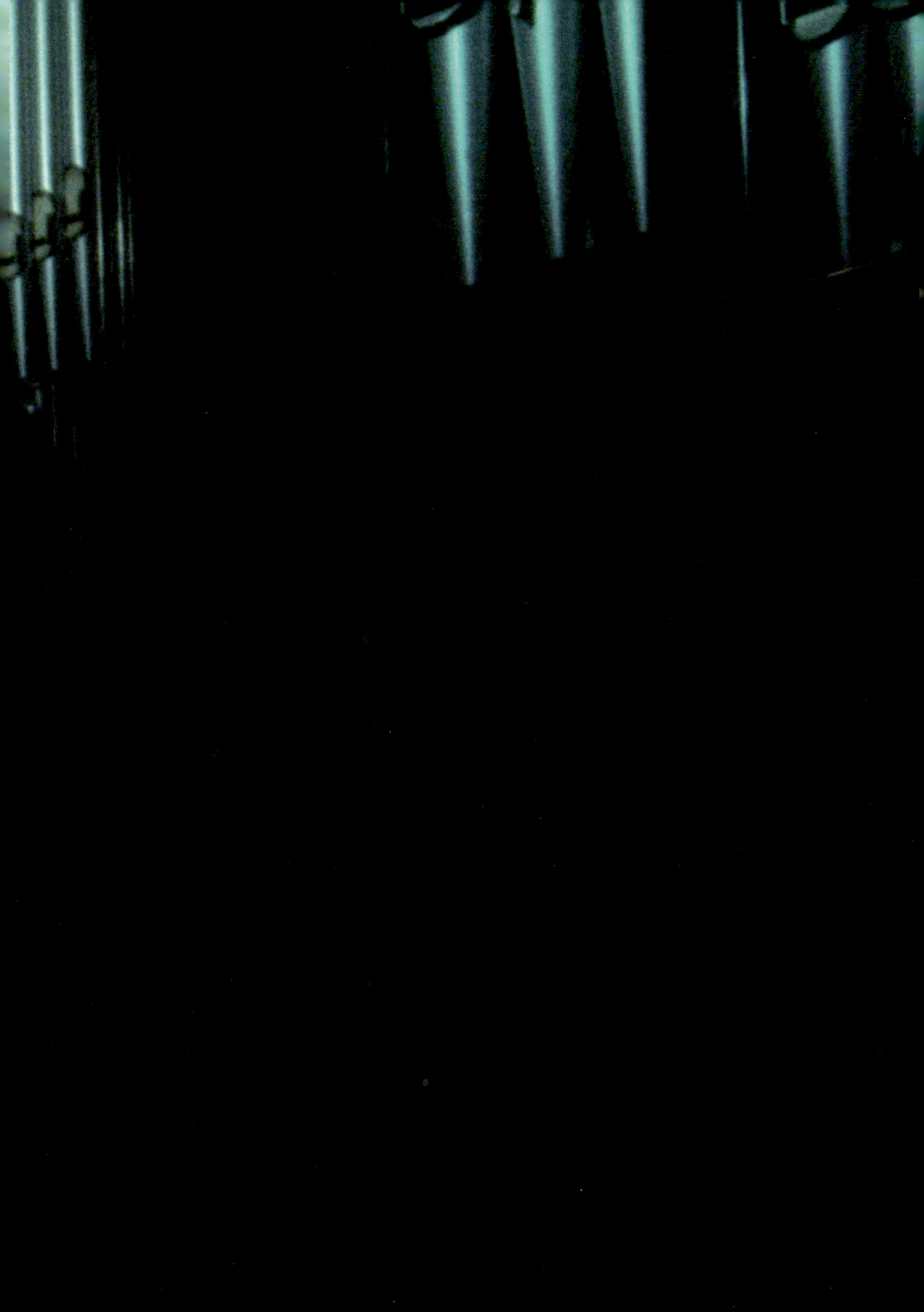

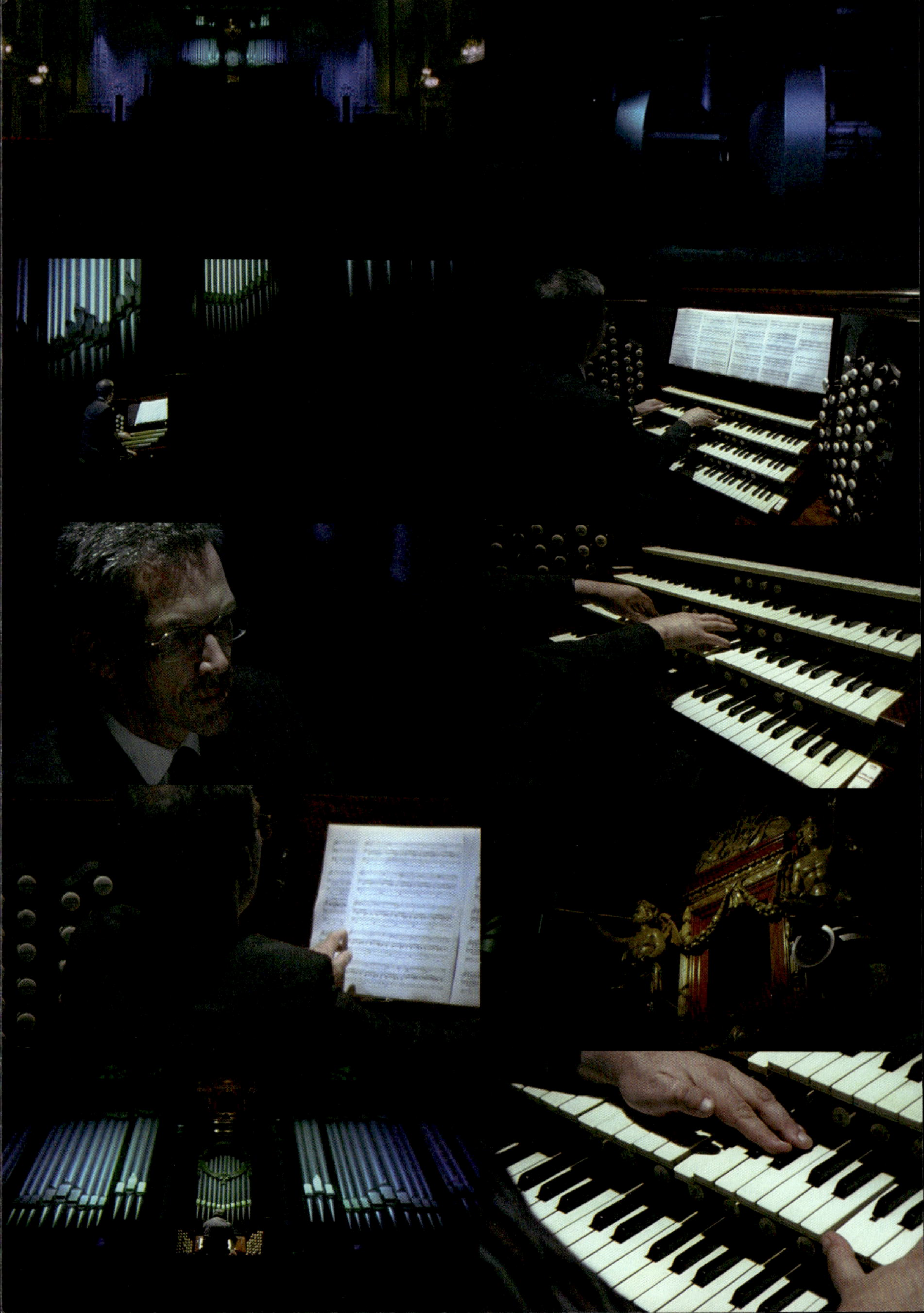

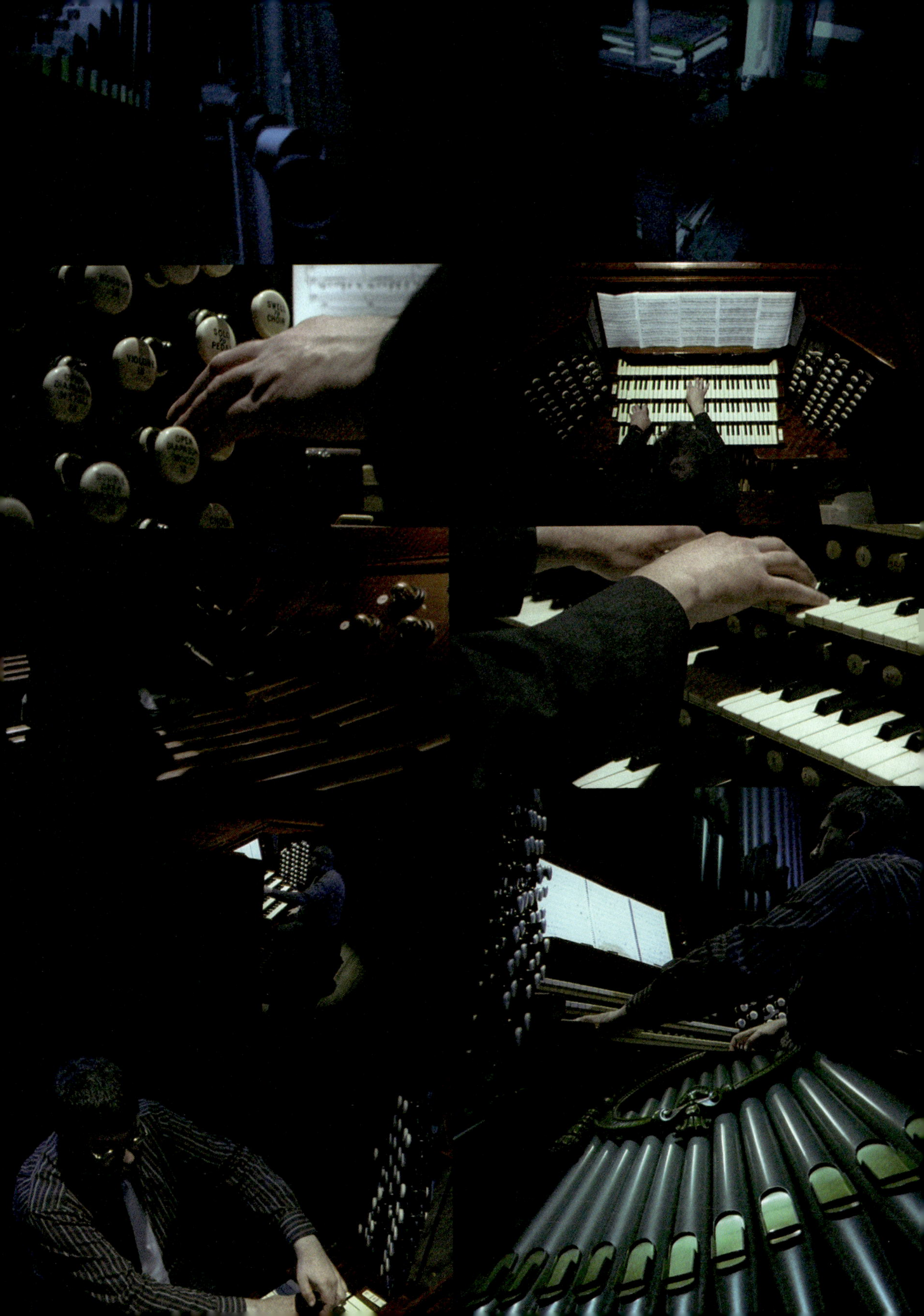

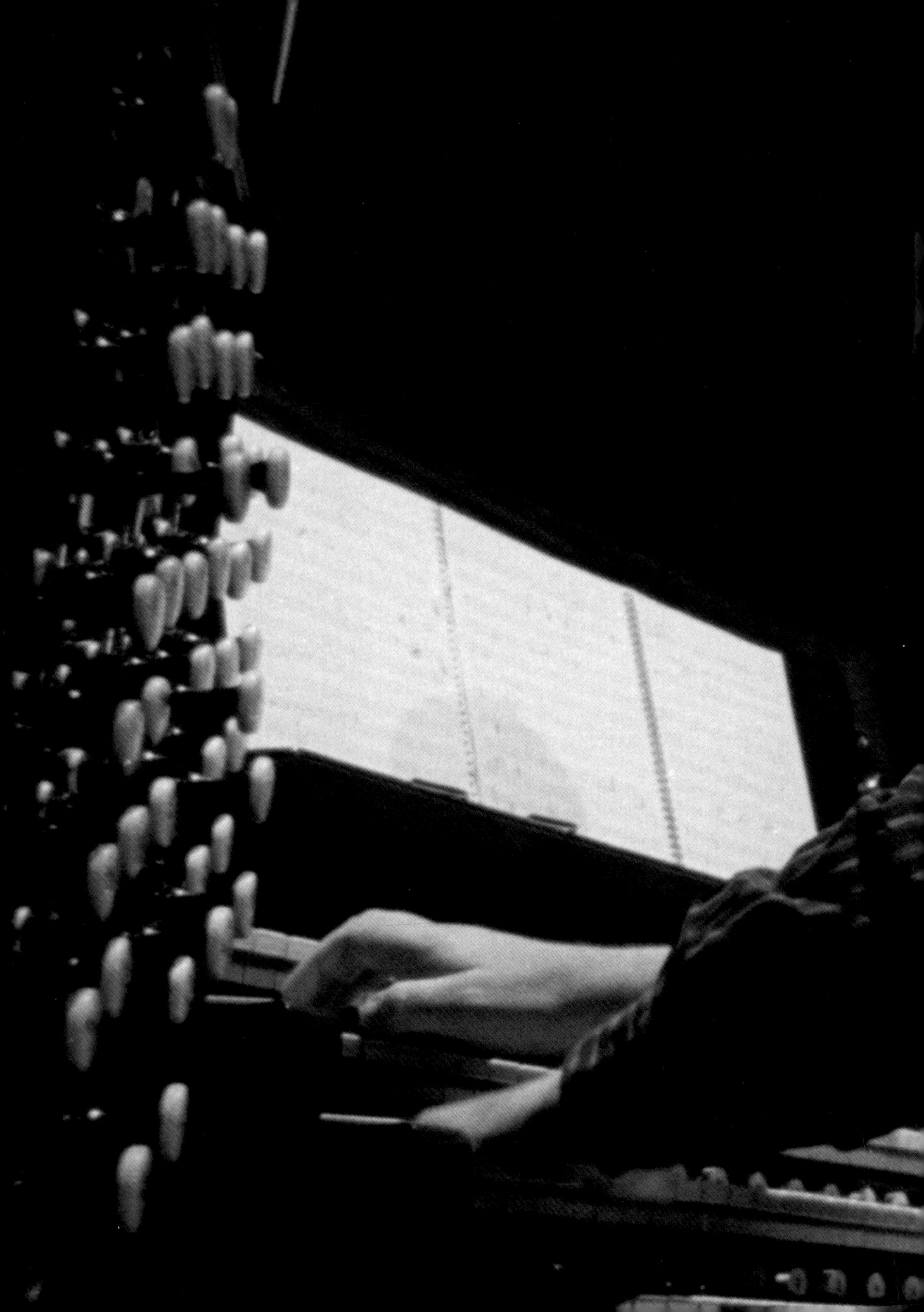

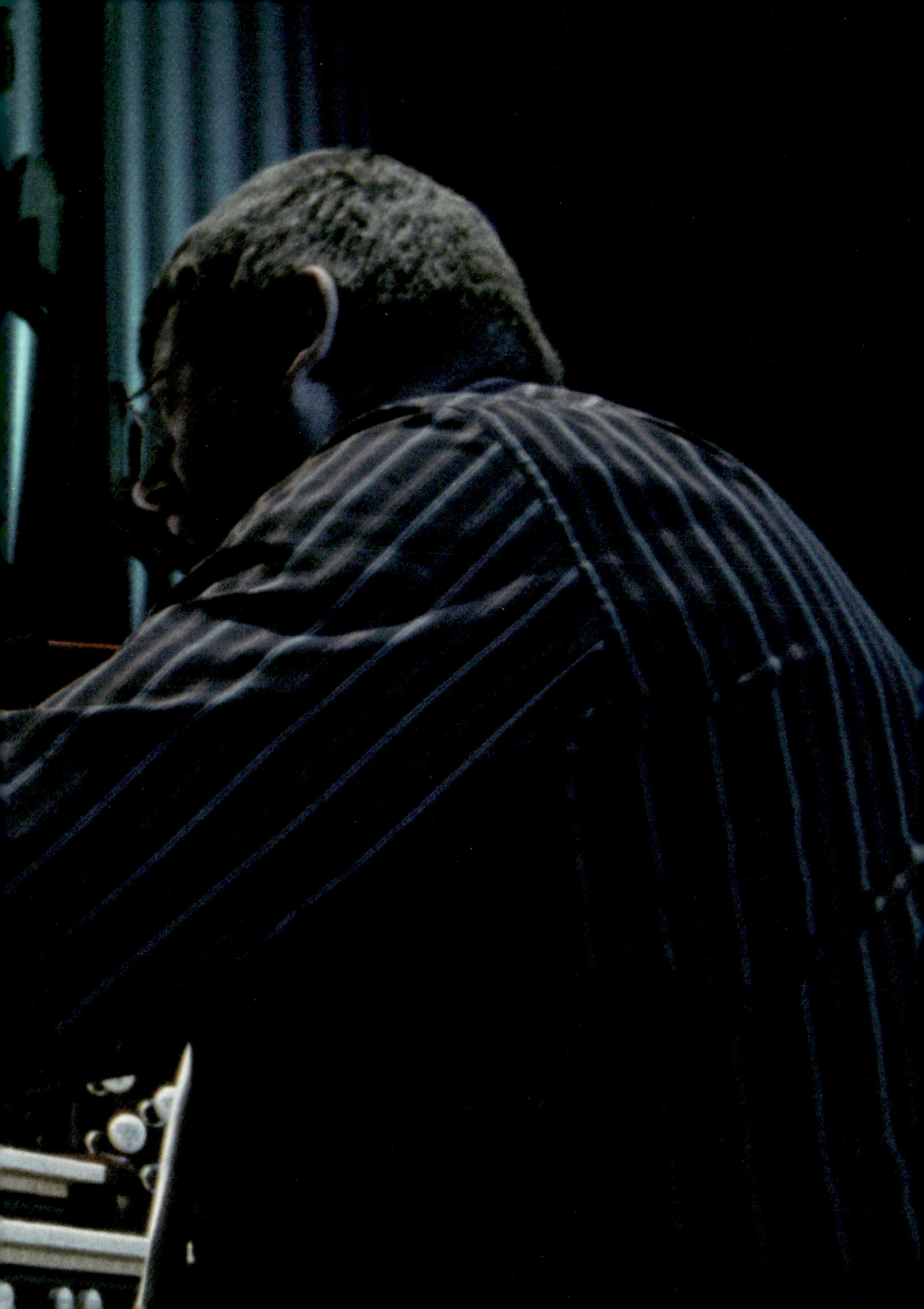

Real Arcadia

Real Arcadia
A research and archive project based on the activities of
Outhouse Promotions, aka the Cave Crew, a defunct Acid House
organisation from the Lake District, England
2003 – ongoing

No Way Back

Matthew Collin

Nervous, pure nervous. A twilit Victorian street in the Lace Market district of Nottingham, at that time still dour and ill-used, a few years away from gentrification. Fear and anticipation. One of us is holding a couple of bottles of cheap supermarket champagne, the other, a small bag of white pills. A siren wails in the distance: we hold still for a second or two, then hurry across the road to the photographic studio in a disused textile factory where we're about to hold our first illegal party. The summer of 1990, only a few days after parliament adopted new legislation to clamp down on outlaw raves. Good timing...

Inside, a sweet surge of electronic noise as the needle falls on the first record – 'LFO' by LFO – and when the bassline drops hard, shuddering through the white room, a feeling of relief and rising joy: it's going to be alright. This is how it started, how it would always start.

The photo studio was a rather conventional venue by the standards of the time. After the Ecstasy-fuelled dance scene began to sweep through Britain in 1988 – 'acid house', we called it then, before it became known as the 'rave scene' and then simply 'dance culture' – people began to search for ever more outlandish places in which to hold illegal parties where they would not be bound by the strictures of Britain's World War One-era licensing laws, which at that time dictated that most nightclubs must close by 2am. So they occupied derelict warehouses, farmers' fields, aircraft hangars, film studios – anywhere to establish a temporary autonomous zone where time would be suspended in a blissful frenzy of noise, light and writhing bodies. In the case of the outlaw ravers documented in Matt Stokes' **Real Arcadia**, a cave in the Lake District was transformed into a nocturnal Wonderland, something that one of them called 'a nightclub in a mountain', but which was so much more than that to many of those whose lives it touched.

Rave culture moved into spaces abandoned during the recession of the 1980s, when Britain's manufacturing industries were devastated. Industrial towns in decline became techno meccas, like Blackburn, the focus of the illegal party scene in the North West due to its abundance of disused factories in which a sound system and lights could be quickly and cheaply installed. Locks cracked, power on, people in; and then in the morning a quick escape into the breaking daylight as if nothing had ever happened. The illegality was part of the thrill, and it felt like some kind of victory when the flash of blue lights didn't bring the music to an untimely end.

Media reports in the late 1980s likened the M25 motorway which encircles London, to a kind of carousel of oblivion, a merry-go-round from which ravers would spin off, hurtling down country lanes, towards parties deep in the Home Counties, only discovering the secret location at the last minute through frantic calls to the organisers from roadside telephone boxes (at that time, mobile phones were relatively new, expensive and rare). It was hard to match the experience of rolling to the peak of some rural hill, to see lasers strafing the darkened skyline and hear the soft thunder of sub-bass rhythms; a fairground big wheel spinning its glow through the darkness, behind it the black tower of speakers already pulsing with sound… and the promise of a long night's journey into dawn…

But while the huge, spectacular events, with their 'top DJs', 'blinding lasers' and 'turbo sound systems' (as the technicolor flyers used to say) were staged close to Britain's biggest cities, people were doing things for themselves on a much more personal and altruistic level all around Britain, putting on small parties which were often free, or subsidised by drug sales. Like the Cave Raves, they didn't achieve national notoriety, although they became a vital focus for emerging alternative cultures in their areas. They were products of sheer enthusiasm, attempts to democratise metropolitan bohemia by taking electronic music and psychedelic drug culture into the heartland of the 'beer monster' and the ritzy discotheque. Or so many thought at the time.

Yet more parties took place in far less glamorous surroundings: the back rooms of pubs or high street nightclubs whose tacky décor and dodgy names still reflected their origins in pre-Ecstasy, six-pints-and-a-Bacardi-and-coke nightlife. When the Cave Crew weren't raving in the quarry, they frequented the rather more traditional surroundings of places like the Stag's Head pub in Bowness-on-Windermere. This was hardly unusual. People would drive for miles around the Midlands and the North West to pack into a glitzy discotheque called Shelleys in Stoke-on-Trent; a venue called The Osbourne in Manchester which looked like a working men's club and became a notorious techno sweatbox known as The Thunderdome; even the first Acid House club in Britain, The Project, was held at an unremarkable suburban 'nitespot' in an unfashionable district of south London. In between the rave spectaculars, the party had to go on. Intoxicated by the moment, nobody wanted the music to stop – it felt somehow as necessary as a heartbeat, and just about anywhere would do. There seemed to be, as Hunter S. Thompson once said about 1960s California, madness at any hour, in any direction.

It was a time of profound optimism, and profound derangement. The names of some of the raves tell the story: Sunrise, Live the Dream, Fantazia, The Trip, Apocalypse Now. Normal rules seemed to be suspended – an impression heightened by drugs, youthful innocence and the sense of belonging to some kind of secret society. Stokes' interviews for **Real Arcadia** capture comments which could have been made by so many others over the decade: 'You know like when you were a kid and you go up to someone in the playground and you'd say "alright mate, what's your name, what do you do, where do you come from..." And that's what it was like. There were no inhibitions whatsoever... everyone was on the same level, and everyone was really happy...' It was a feeling that many thought would last forever – although of course it could not and did not.

Rave culture was rooted in new technologies – musical and chemical – but it also sampled and remixed ideas, as well as sounds, from a variety of Pop-cult sources: the Saturday Night Fever traditions of gay Disco and the Amphetamine-fuelled Northern Soul scene, the do-it-yourself ethics of Punk, and vague hippy philosophies handed down from 1960s psychedelia (although cut loose from the protest politics of that era). However, it could not help but reflect the time of its birth, at the high watermark of Thatcherite free-market materialism: this was an entrepreneurial culture which was energised by the small-time business activities of party promoters, record producers and drug dealers.

And yet while the rave scene enthusiastically embraced Margaret Thatcher's urge to entrepreneurialism, it implicitly rejected her assertion that there was 'no such thing as society'. It was driven by a deep and powerful desire not only for transcendence, but also for community: to be part of something greater, a feeling amplified by the empathy-enhancing effects of Ecstasy. There was also a widespread desire for it to 'mean something', although nobody could really give a convincing explanation of exactly *what* it meant, and the search for meaning was in some cases little more than a human need to rationalise what seemed to be such a momentous experience. Hence some of the myths that grew up around Ecstasy, like the suggestion that it ended the football violence of the 1980s when loved-up hooligans from opposing teams began to hug other each at raves instead of slashing each other with razor-blades, or the belief that it promoted multi-cultural tolerance.

Effectively, in the absence of any ideological gurus, people brought their own beliefs to the party, and saw the rave scene in terms of those beliefs. So it became home to some dedicated anarchists who believed it was part of a rebel crusade against the capitalist system, and to a few intrepid young Conservatives who saw it as an expression of radical libertarianism – as well as to many more who would speak vaguely about 'sharing' and 'togetherness' and 'love', about celebrating as one, beyond the British divides of class, race and regional origins. However, perhaps for the majority of those involved, there was no attempt at analysis or any need for it: this was simply the most exciting thing that had happened to them in their young lives.

The spectacular rise of this new youth culture was hard to ignore, and inevitably the backlash started almost as quickly as the scene itself, with the first shock-horror newspaper headlines and reports of police raids appearing towards the end of 1988, only a year after the first Acid House parties were held. After that, the outrage flowed in consecutive waves, following the traditional sequence of moral panics about renegade cults corrupting the minds of Britain's youth. First the scandalised press despatches and the calls for 'something to be done', followed by police action and government legislation. But it turned out that much of the agitated media coverage simply acted as an advertisement. All-night dancing, hypnotic rhythms, mind-warping chemicals: many found such sweet but forbidden fruits tempting indeed.

The police were initially caught unprepared by the strange stirrings in the countryside, but eventually they set up specially-equipped units to combat what they prosaically referred to as 'pay parties'. The experience of the Cave Crew in the Lake District was not unusual: concerned reports in local newspapers and on regional television about the threat to young people's safety, then the erection of police roadblocks – 'We are not killjoys, we are trying to preserve life', the words of the local police chief, were typical of the time – and finally the suggestion that the caves should be dynamited to put a stop to the madness. By 1997, parliament had passed three separate pieces of legislation aimed at curbing the wilder excesses of the rave scene. When combined with the introduction of more liberal licensing laws, they contributed to both the ultimate commercialisation of the scene as well as the radicalisation of a small but dedicated outlaw fringe who even now continue to travel the roads staging illegal parties – although none of the new laws would halt the irrepressible growth of Britain's drug culture.

And it was inevitable that any culture based on illegal drug use would have even more serious repercussions – legal, medical and psychological. Many people ended up with criminal records; everyone knew someone who had been arrested after being caught with a bag of pills, and those who thought they were simply helping friends to have a good night out soon realised that the law regarded them as drug dealers like any others. The fact that Ecstasy was illegal also attracted those who could organise large-scale imports of the drug: serious criminals, men with weapons and few scruples, and – as in the case of the Cave Raves – low-life thugs wielding baseball bats who wanted to make a little easy cash by using their muscle to 'tax' illicit parties. Yet few wanted to talk about the criminal empires which were being built upon their pleasures.

The drug itself had its own complications too; although Ecstasy wasn't addictive, for some people it represented an introduction to the wider world of recreational chemistry. Some ravers who chased the buzz a little too hard developed psychological problems – 'lost it', to use the slang of the time – and a few, endlessly seeking the next rush, became addicted to Heroin.

But then there was worse: some time around the start of the 1990s, it became clear that small but significant numbers of people were dying after taking Ecstasy, mainly people in their teens or early twenties who thought they were about to have the time of their lives but ended up in the ground. Many ravers were reluctant to blame their beloved, life-affirming 'happy pills', pointing out that most of those who died had expired through heatstroke after not drinking enough water. But the fact remained that if they hadn't gone out and taken Ecstasy, they would probably still be alive. Year by year, a little more innocence was lost. The story of the Cave Raves, again, serves as a kind of parable for these times: some of the people connected with the Lake District party crew have since served prison time. One is dead.

The dance scene reached its peak as a mass movement sometime in the mid-1990s. But apart from fuelling a mass drug culture in Britain which continued to grow even afterwards, its legacy remains hazy and difficult to assess, particularly for those who were involved. There is the music, of course, captured in hundreds of wonderful recordings and thousands more dreadful ones. There are the careers in pop culture and media which grew out of the scene. There was the development of computer-aided do-it-yourself creativity and spontaneous, *ad hoc* networking which fed into the obsessions of the internet age, while the technology used by outlaw raves was deployed with more serious intent by the environmental road-protest movement of the 1990s.

And yet even now, two decades after the first Acid House record sounded its urgent call to action, the lingering question – 'so what did it all mean?' – still evades an answer. 'They were special times, really special times', one of the Cave Crew says – but was that all that they were? Many people went through life-changing experiences – they are the ones who still glow with nostalgia while talking about how they discovered new ways of seeing the world, found routes out of dead-end jobs, forged new friendships and relationships. But others will speak of mental illness, prison and death, and it's no surprise that some of the people who Stokes tried to contact for **Real Arcadia** simply didn't want to talk about those times again: for whatever reason, they didn't want to remember. And then there are those who say it was nothing more than youthful hedonism, a necessarily limited period of liberty before entering the adult world of responsibilities and obligations.

But perhaps what it really 'meant' can never be captured in words – and to do so would only devalue the intensity of that indefinable feeling. Perhaps it was no more than a moment of pure communal abandon, lost in the music with no way back, transported into raptures beyond rational thought. Perhaps that, in itself, was more than we ever could have hoped for.

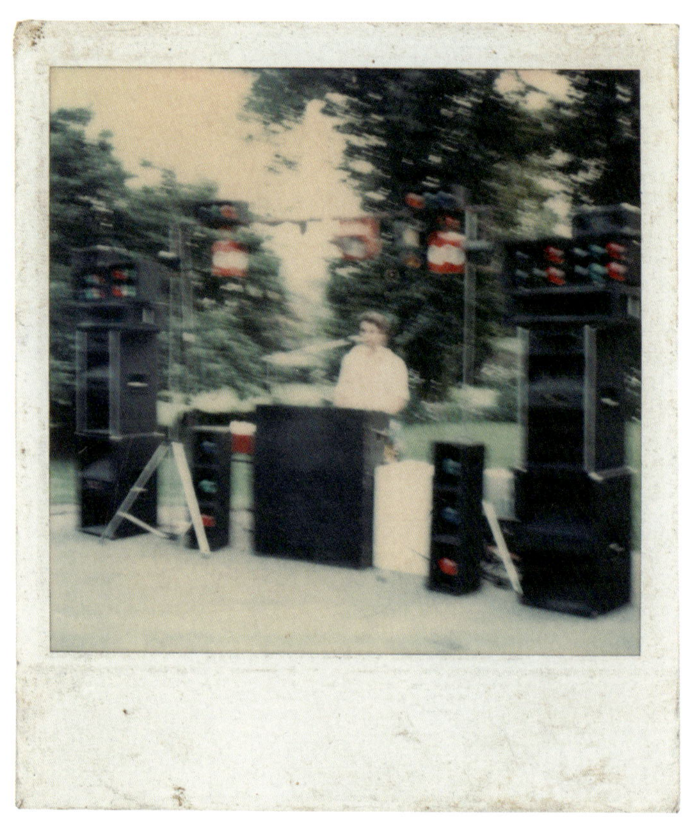

Powie with his mobile disco prior to the formation of Outhouse
Promotions. *c.*1986.

outhouse PROMOTIONS

fOR fREE MEMbERsHIP & DETaIls of fUTURE RaVES
sEND a S • A • E • to :—
oUTHOUSE PROMoTIoNs, THE HOllIEs,
MIllER BRIDGE, AMBlEsiDE, CUMBRia.

outhouse PROMOTIONS

fOR fREE MEMbERsHIP & DETaIls of fUTURE RaVES
sEND a S • A • E • to :—
oUTHOUSE PROMoTIoNs, THE HOllIEs,
MIllER BRIDGE, AMBlEsiDE, CUMBRia.

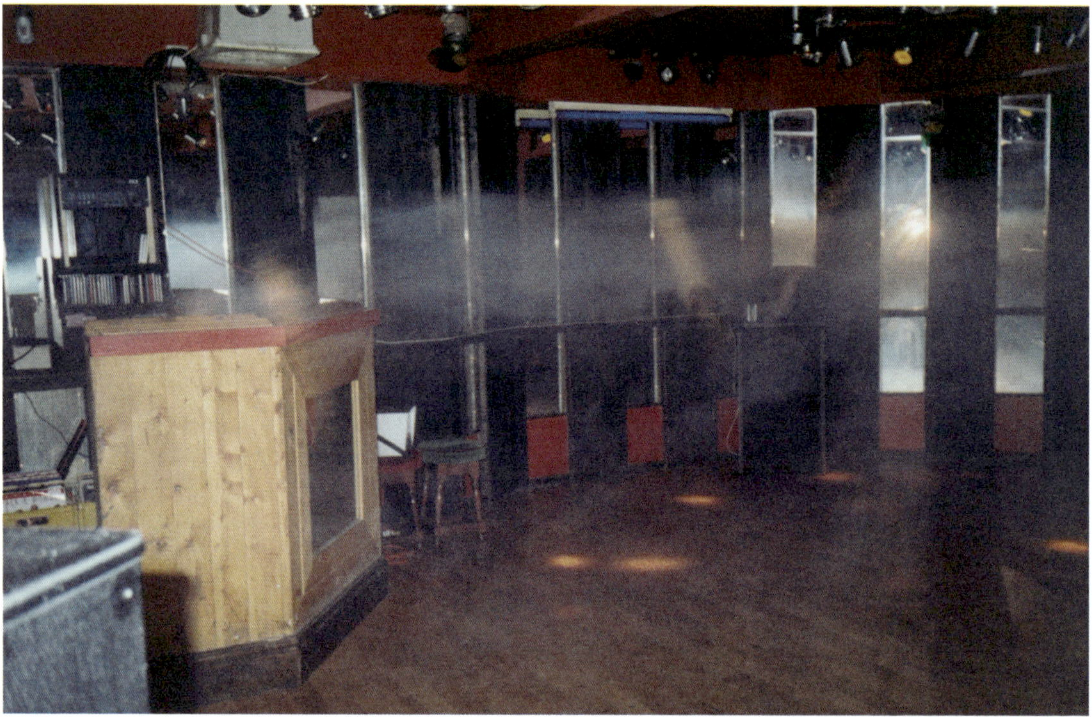

Basement club at the Stag's Head, Bowness-on-Windermere. *c.*1988.

Steely D's Vauxhall Cavalier and Ohm speakers. 1989.

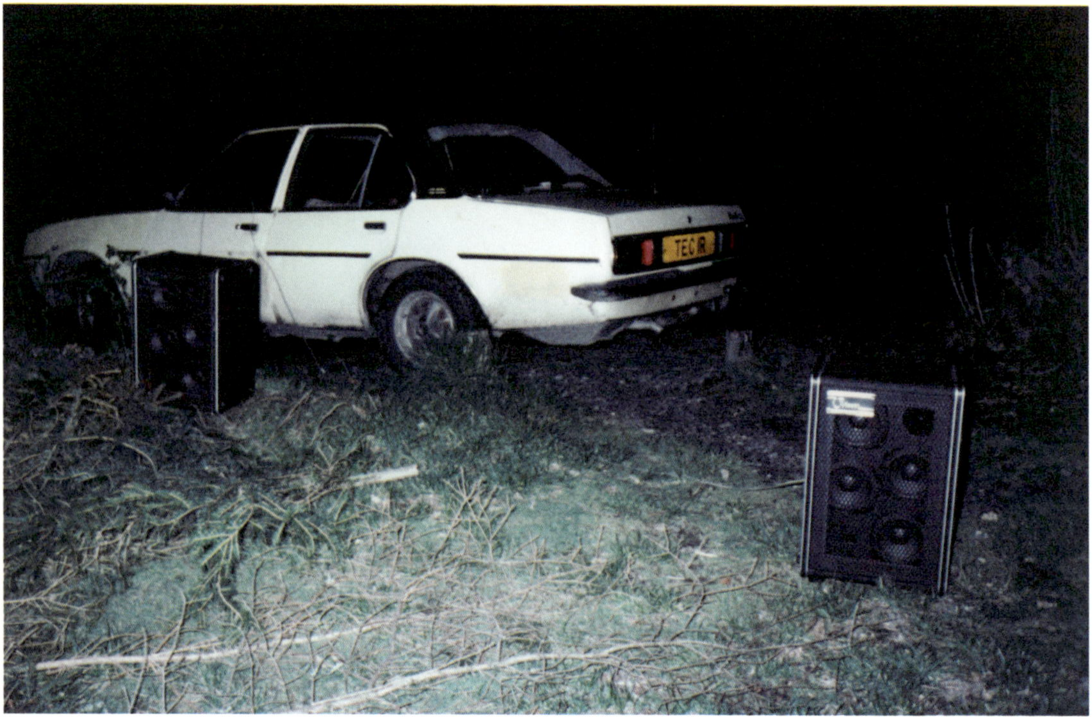

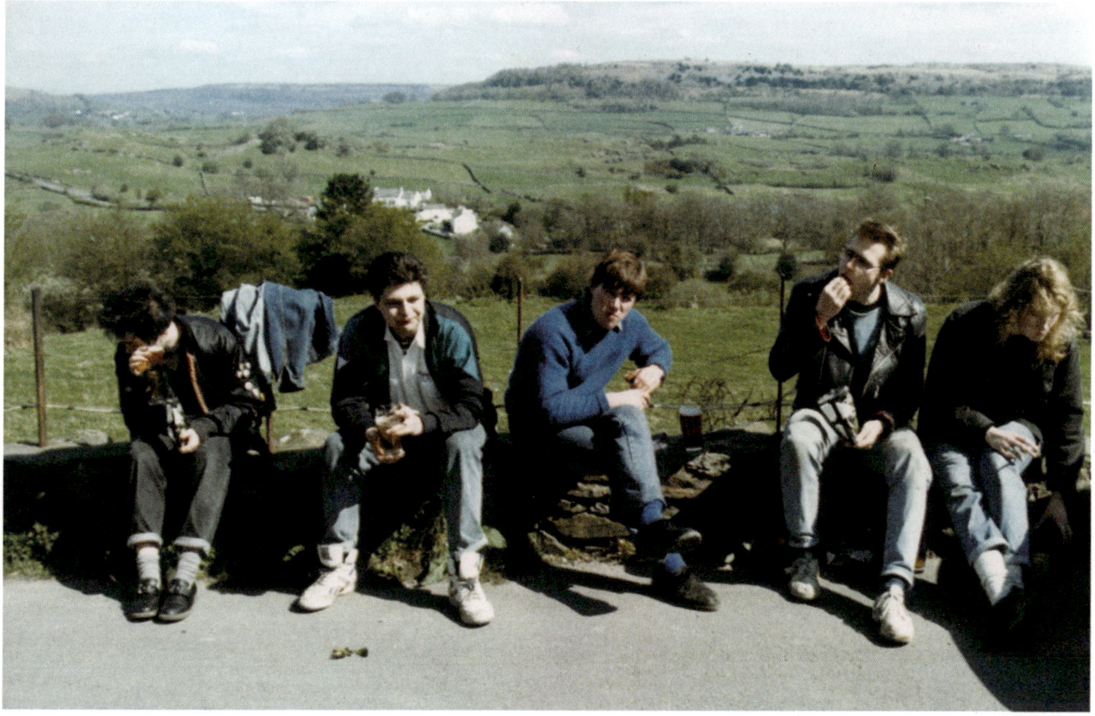

Outhouse and friends at Strawberry Bank, Cumbria. 1989.

Grog. 1989.

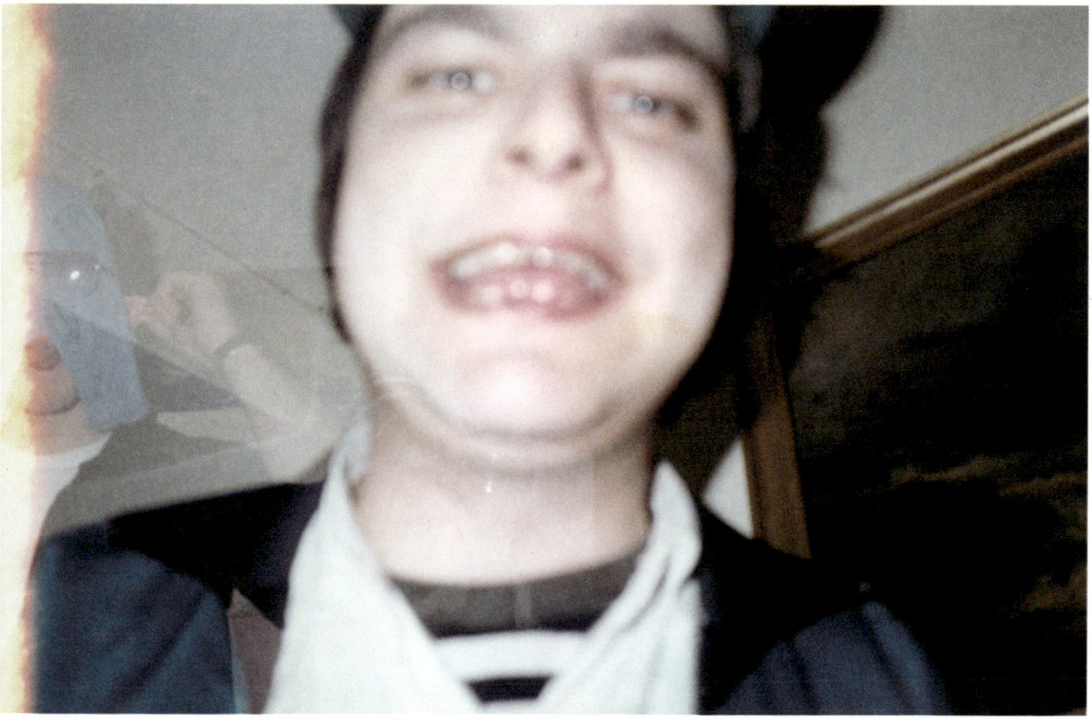

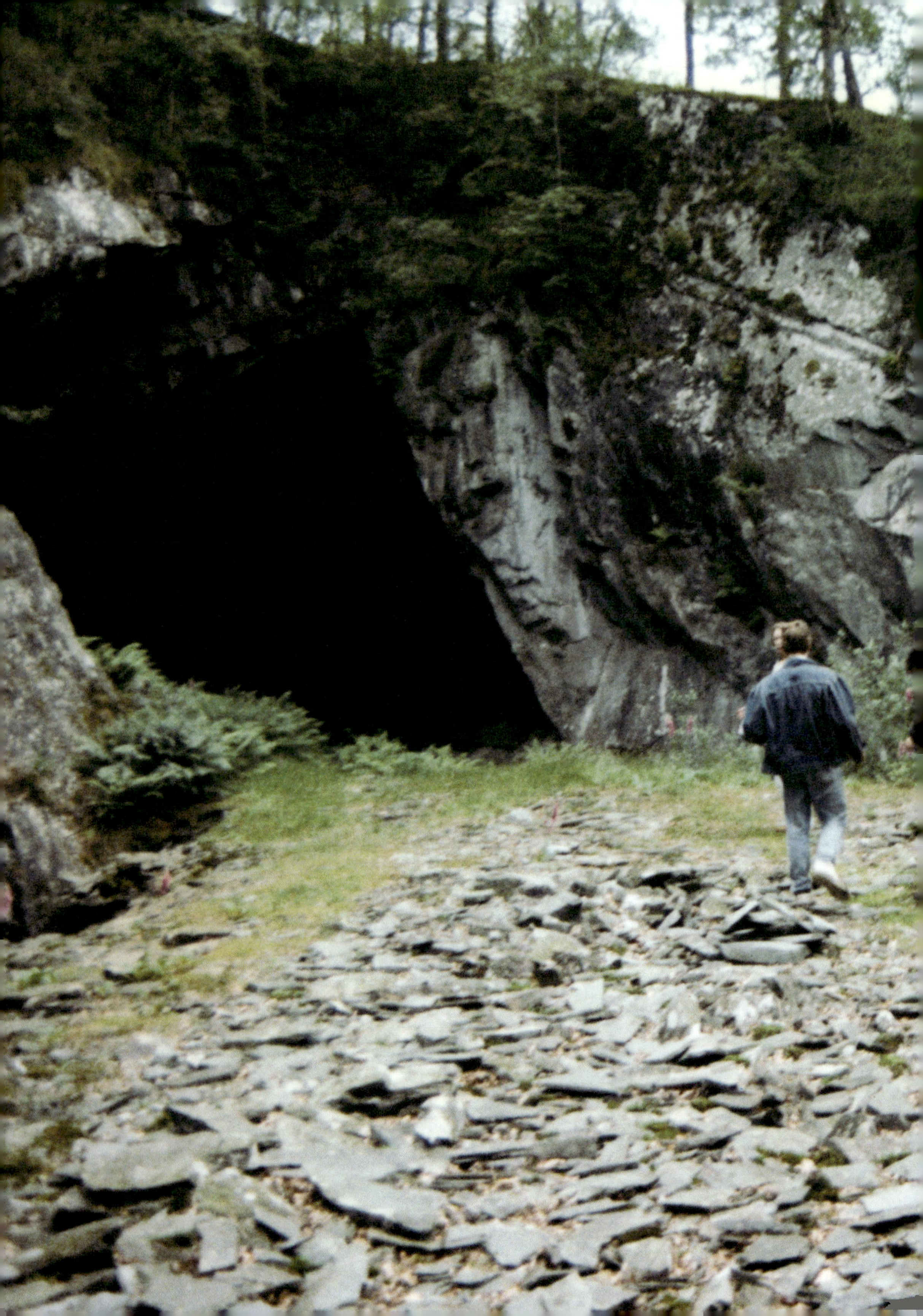

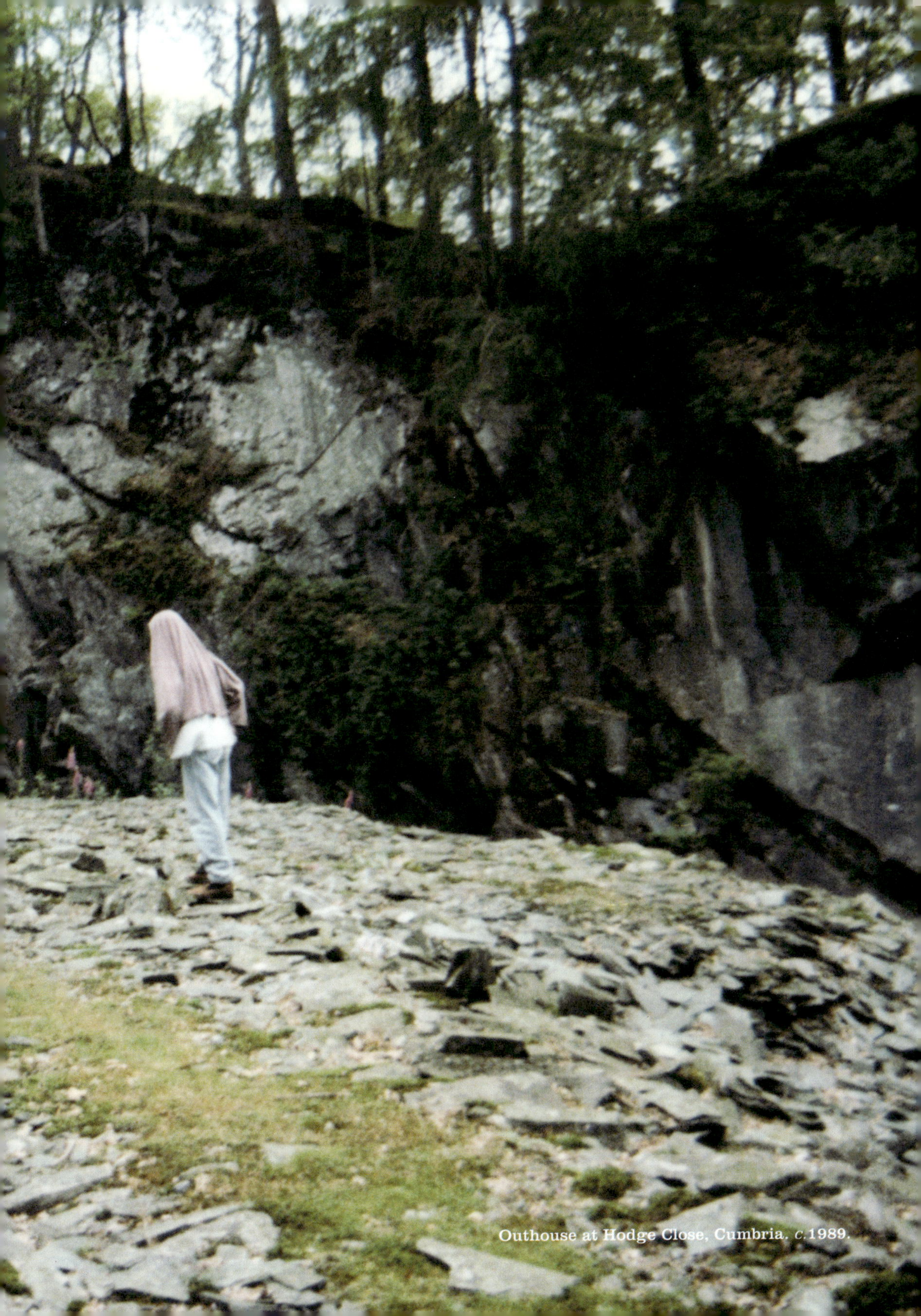

Outhouse at Hodge Close, Cumbria. *c.*1989.

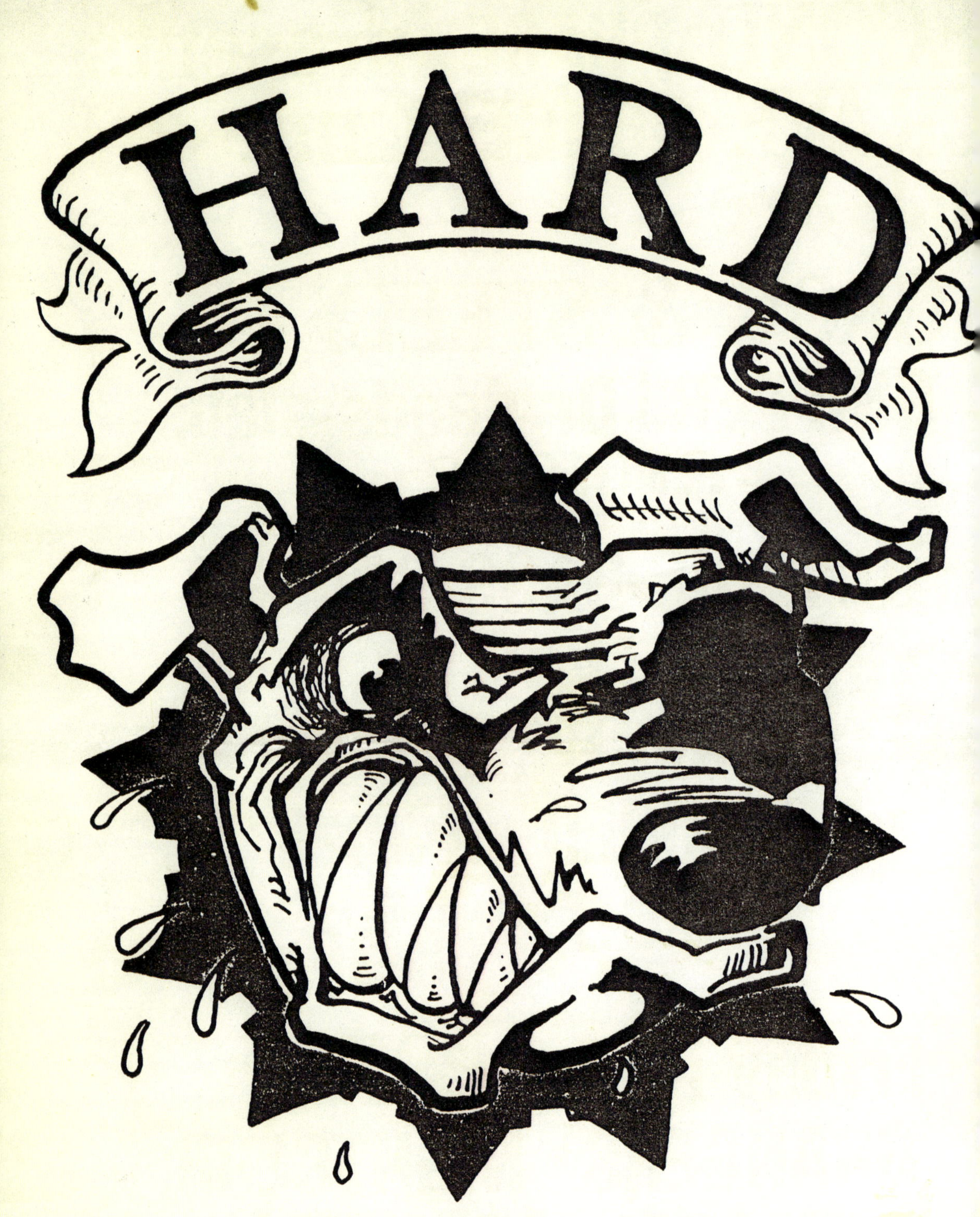

HARD

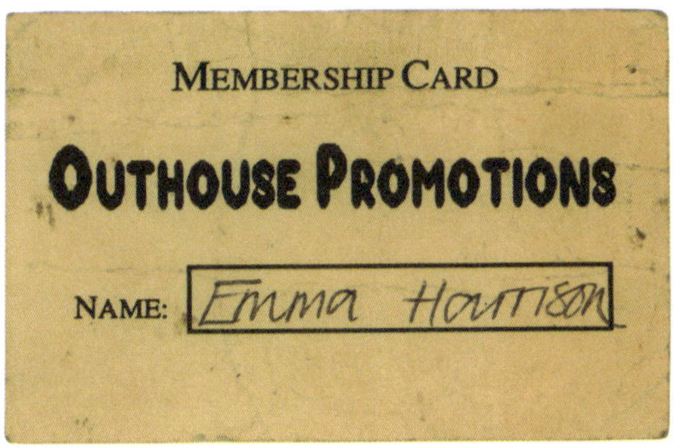

MEMBERSHIP CARD
OUTHOUSE PROMOTIONS
NAME: Emma Harrison

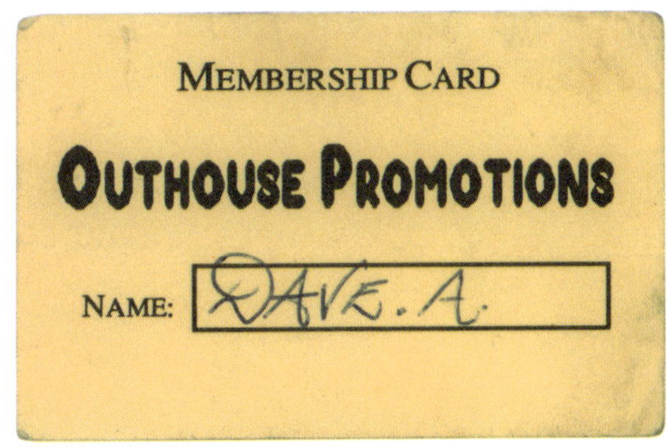

MEMBERSHIP CARD
OUTHOUSE PROMOTIONS
NAME: DAVE.A.

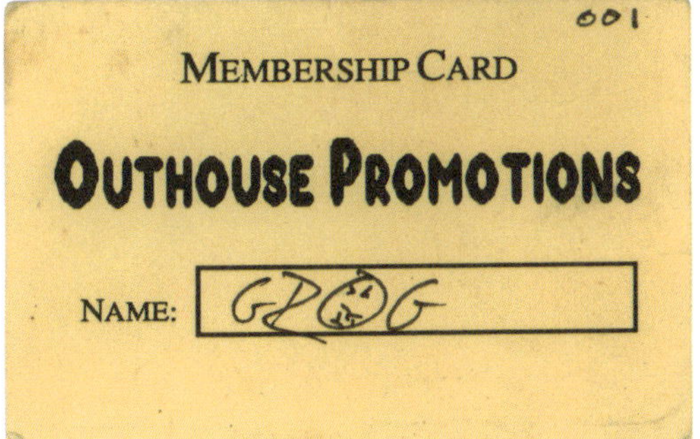

001
MEMBERSHIP CARD
OUTHOUSE PROMOTIONS
NAME: GROG

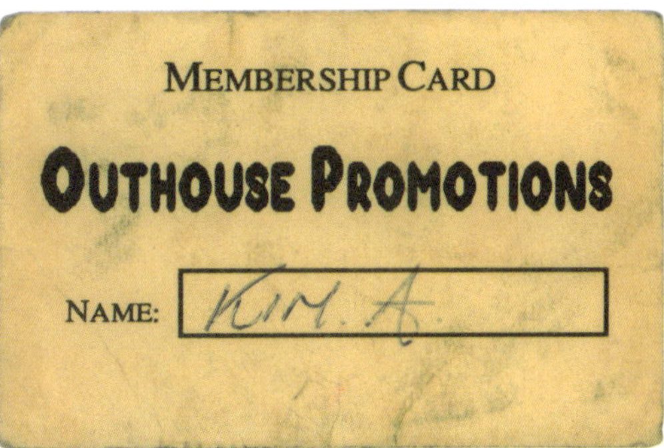

MEMBERSHIP CARD
OUTHOUSE PROMOTIONS
NAME: KIM.A.

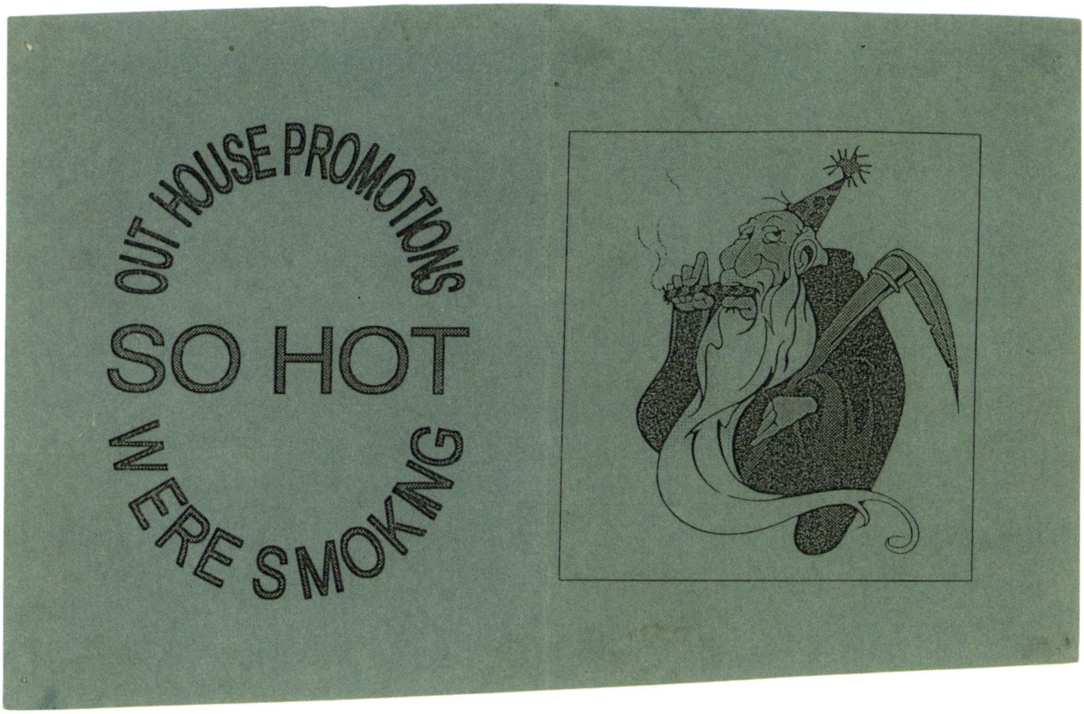

OUT HOUSE PROMOTIONS
SO HOT
WE'RE SMOKING

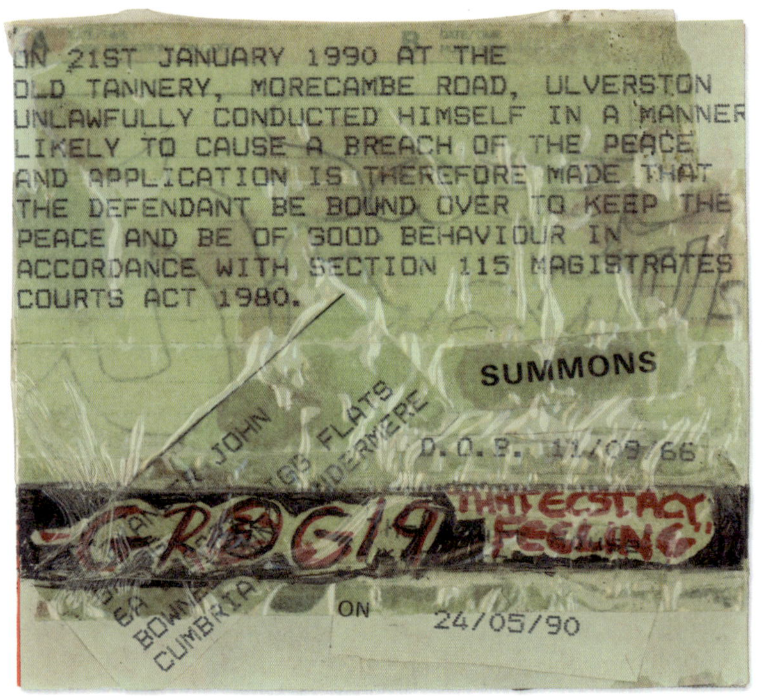
ON 21ST JANUARY 1990 AT THE
OLD TANNERY, MORECAMBE ROAD, ULVERSTON
UNLAWFULLY CONDUCTED HIMSELF IN A MANNER
LIKELY TO CAUSE A BREACH OF THE PEACE
AND APPLICATION IS THEREFORE MADE THAT
THE DEFENDANT BE BOUND OVER TO KEEP THE
PEACE AND BE OF GOOD BEHAVIOUR IN
ACCORDANCE WITH SECTION 115 MAGISTRATES
COURTS ACT 1980.
SUMMONS
D.O.B. 11/09/66
ON 24/05/90

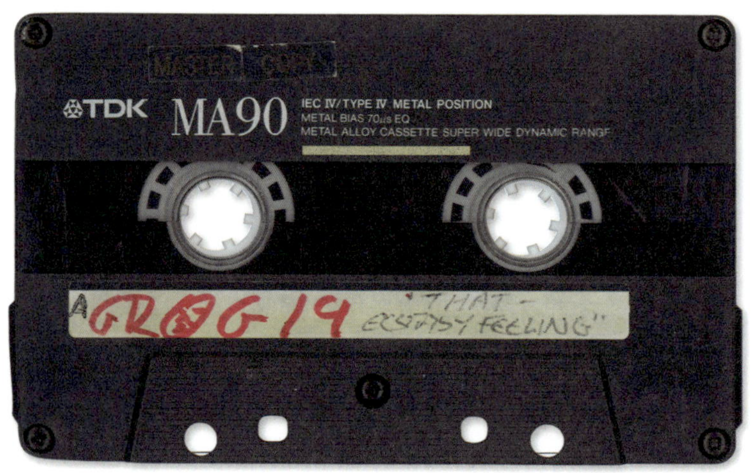
TDK MA90
IEC IV/TYPE IV METAL POSITION
METAL BIAS 70μs EQ
METAL ALLOY CASSETTE SUPER WIDE DYNAMIC RANGE
A GROG 19 "THAT ECSTASY FEELING"

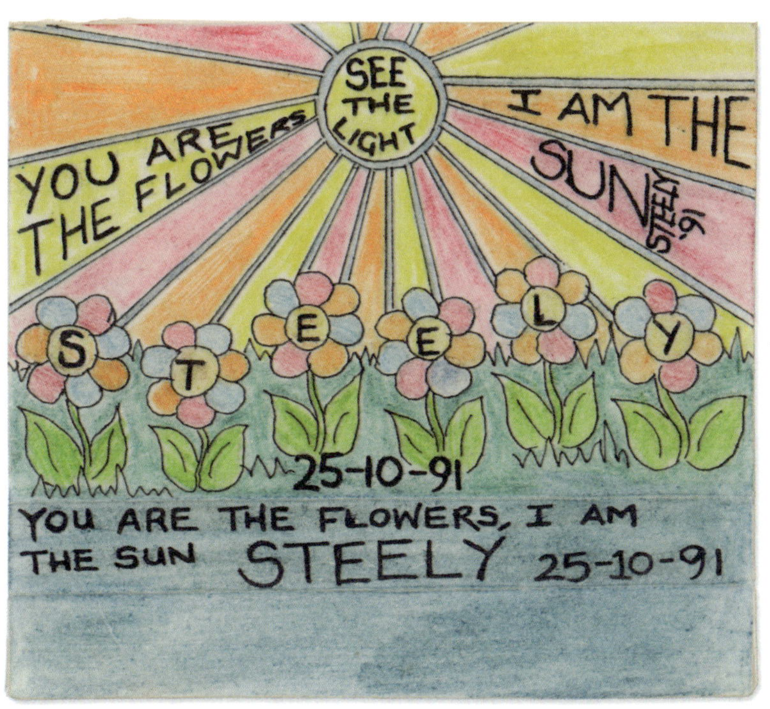

SEE THE LIGHT
YOU ARE THE FLOWERS
I AM THE SUN
STEELY '91
S T E E L Y
25-10-91
YOU ARE THE FLOWERS, I AM THE SUN STEELY 25-10-91

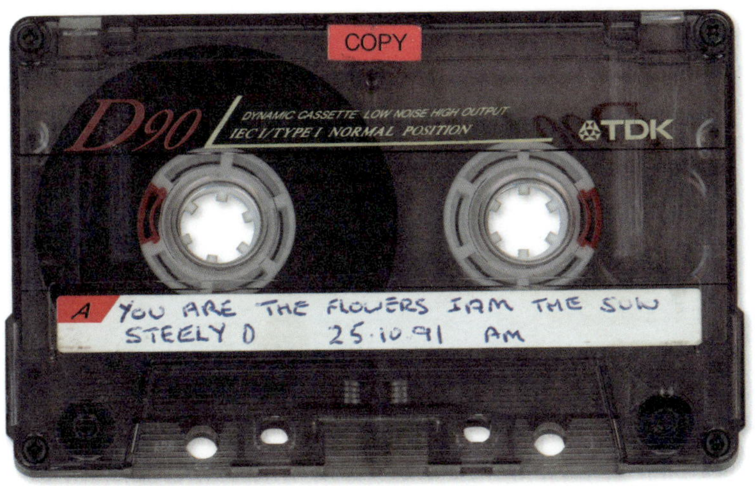

COPY
D90 DYNAMIC CASSETTE LOW NOISE HIGH OUTPUT
IEC I/TYPE I NORMAL POSITION
TDK
A YOU ARE THE FLOWERS IAM THE SUN
STEELY O 25·10·91 AM

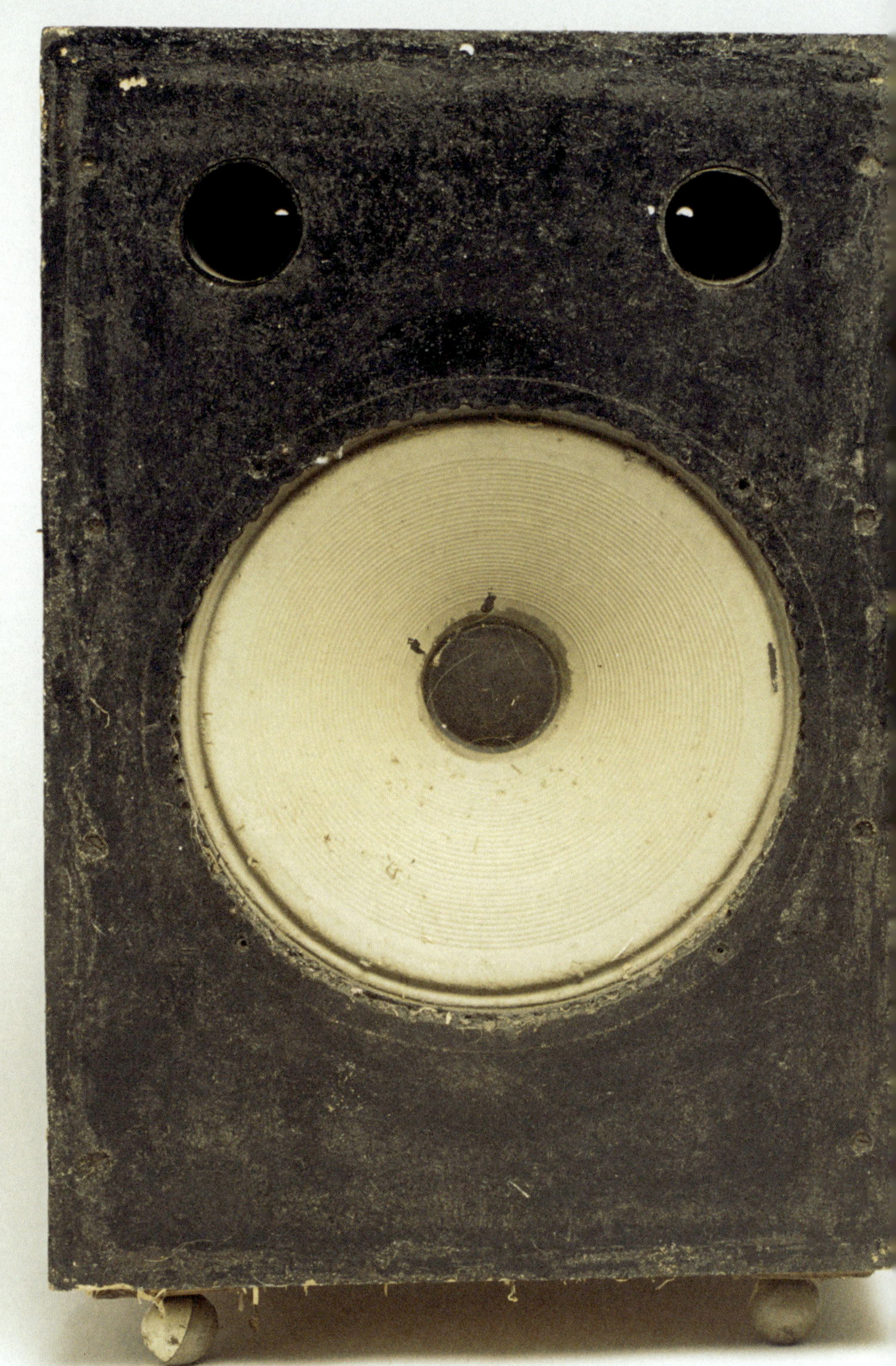

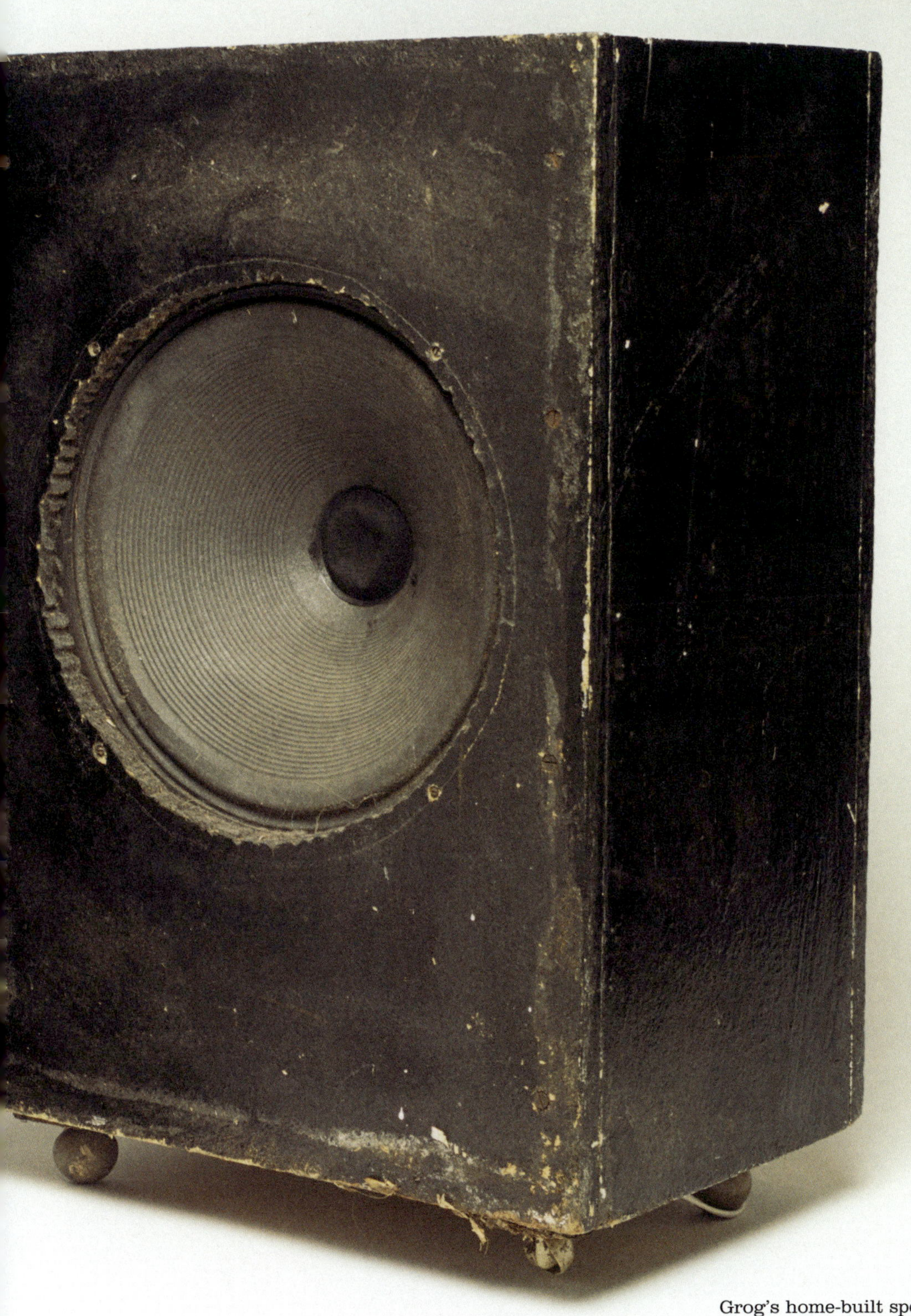

Grog's home-built speakers

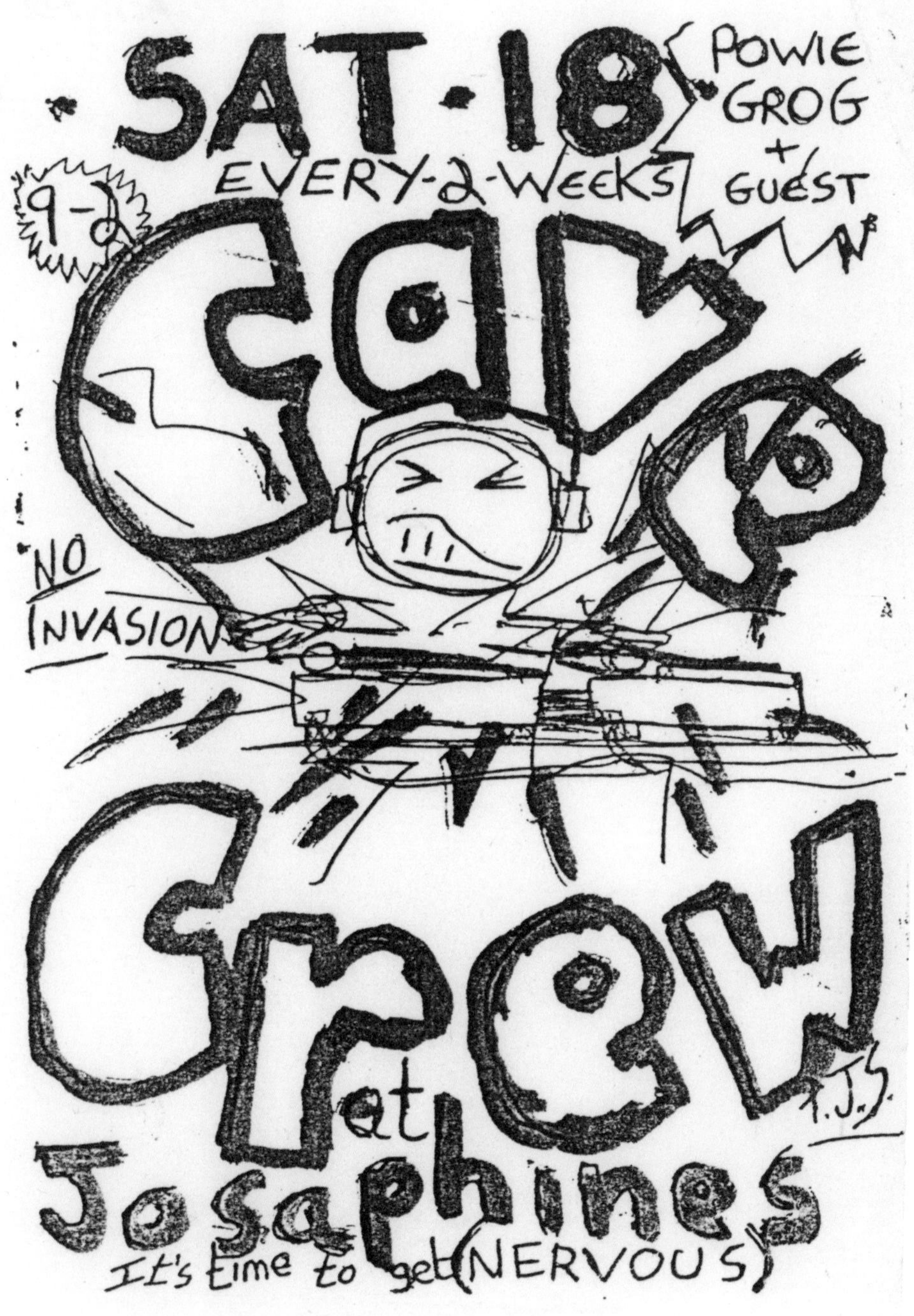

SAT · 18
9 - 2
EVERY · 2 · WEEKS
POWIE GROG + GUEST
CAV
NO INVASION
Crew
at
Josaphines
It's time to get NERVOUS

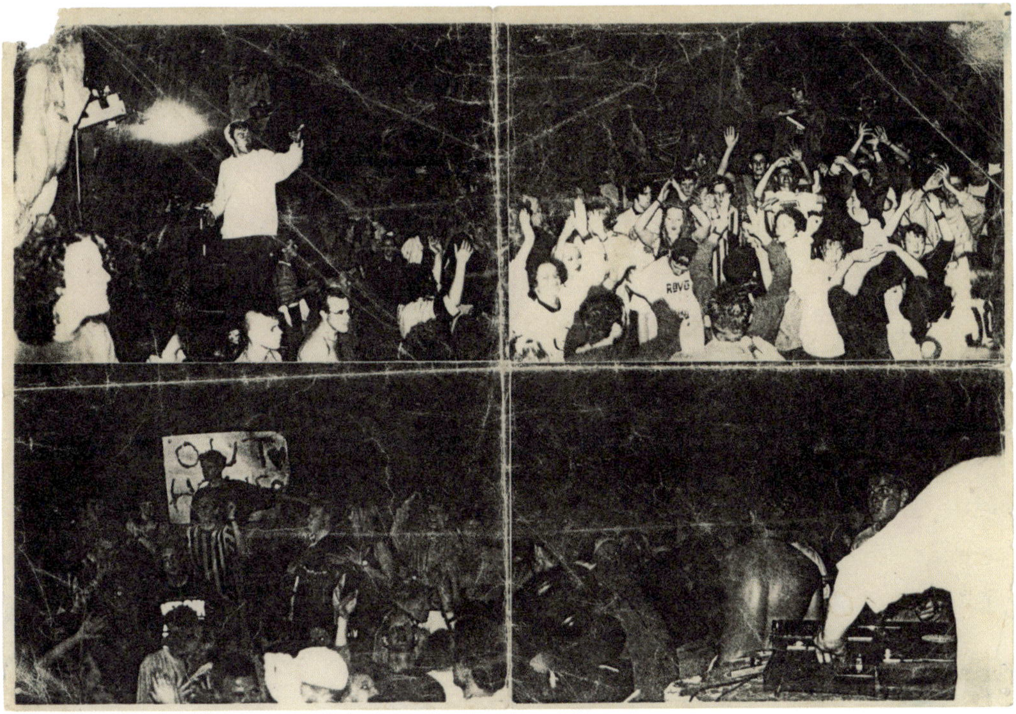

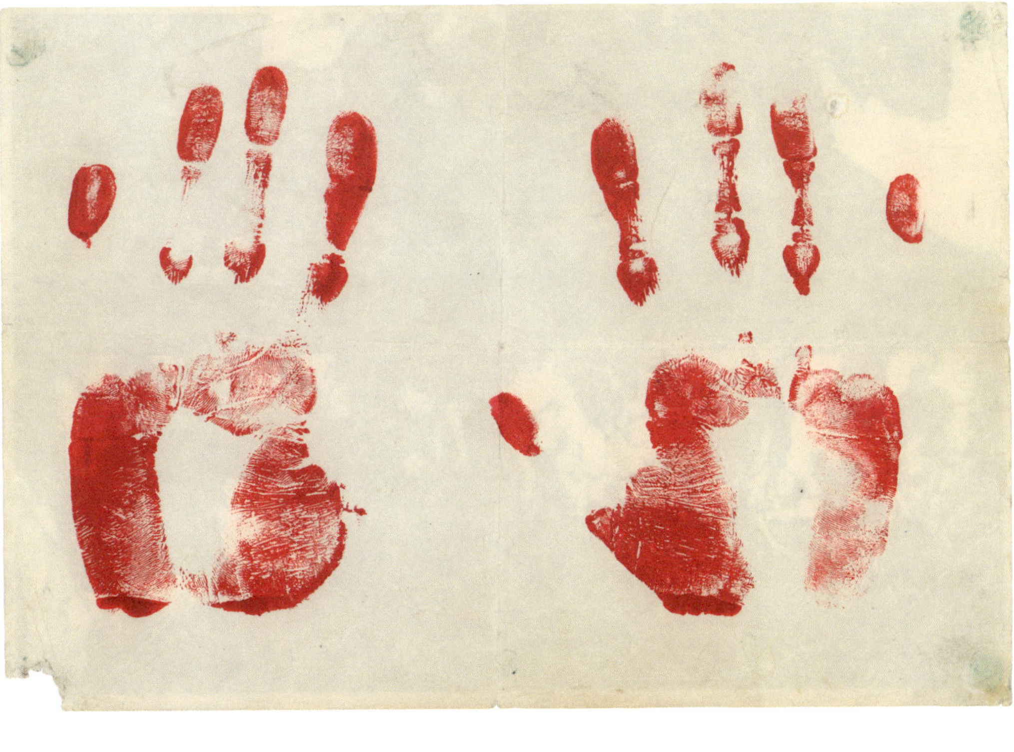

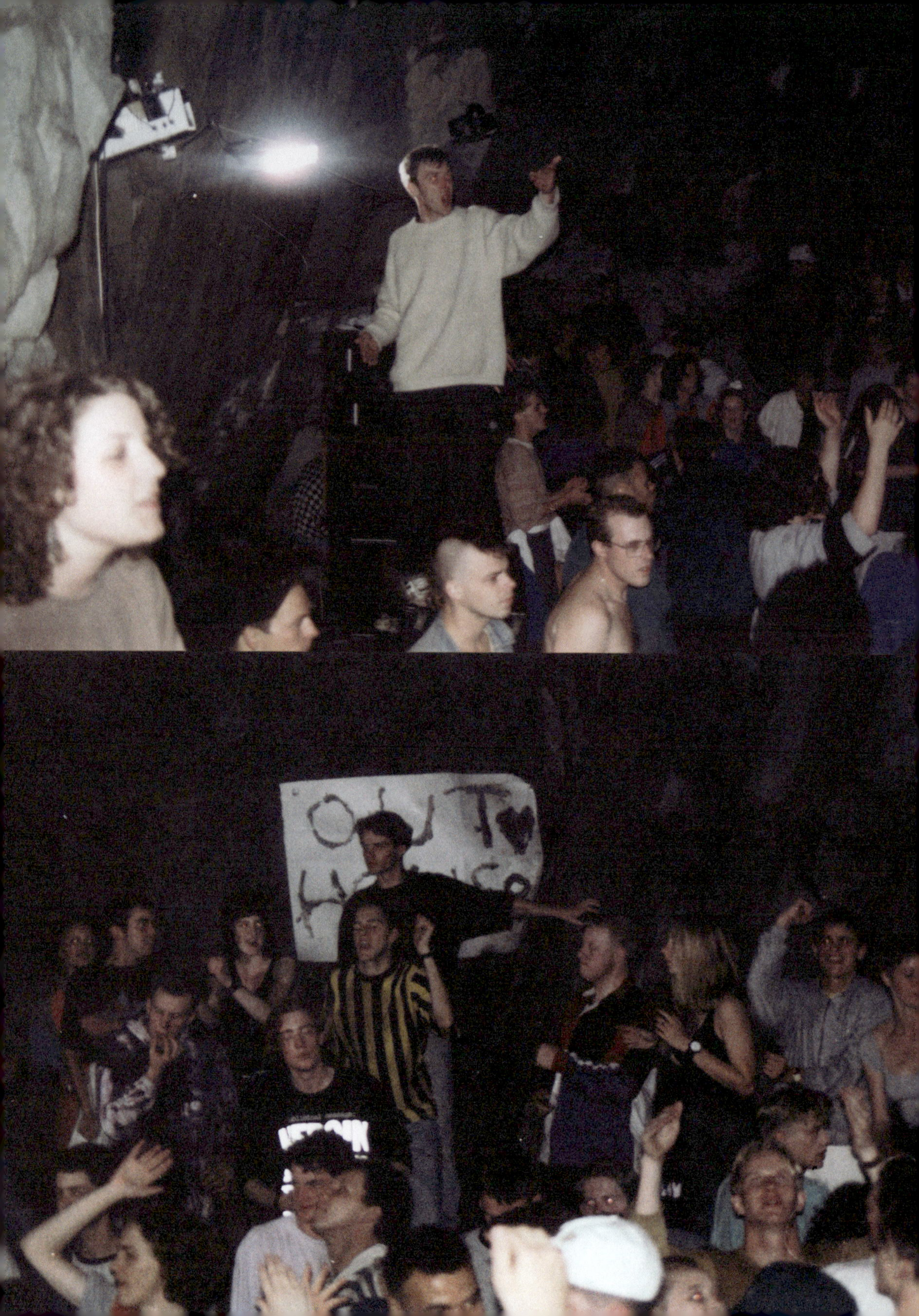

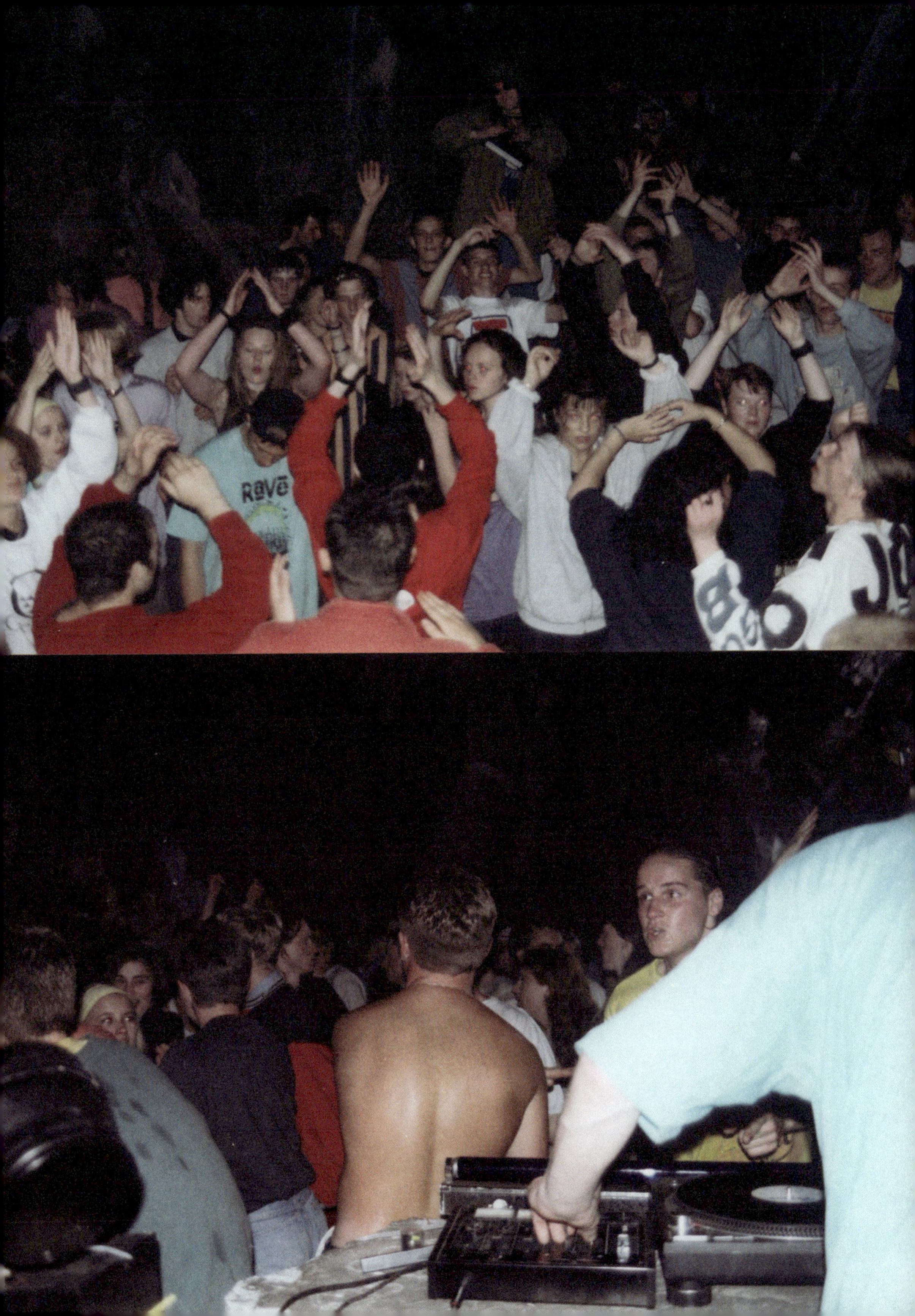

Cave raves defended

Organisers of rave parties held in caves at Hodge Close, Coniston, say the events are perfectly legal. But police have repeated warnings about potential dangers after a diver drowned in the water-filled quarry, **reports Joanne Colley**.

Hitting back at claims that people were "drugged out of their eyeballs", partygoers say police and residents were guilty of gross exaggeration.

In last week's Westmorland Gazette, police and land agents said they wanted a stop put to the parties because they were afraid someone was going to get killed in the dangerous terrain which includes mine shafts, caverns, drops and deep water.

They were also concerned at reports of participants using drugs.

Nearby residents complained of being kept awake all night by the music, noise and traffic, and said party goers had used their gardens as toilets. One lady had said she found a packet of drugs on her doorstep the morning after a party.

But Windermere DJ David Steel, one of the organisers of the party, said the claims were "cabbubble".

"We were just a few friends, a few local people getting together to have a party.

"There was no charge made for the party so it wasn't illegal and didn't require a public entertainments licence," he told the Gazette.

He said because word got around, a lot of people had turned up from other areas such as Millom and Ulverston.

Mr Steel said that neither he nor his friends took drugs, and they simply wanted to relax and listen to good music.

"The parties are free and a lot of fun. There is nothing like that around here for locals. If you want to go to an all night dance, you have got to go to places like Liverpool.

"I admit that perhaps the traffic could be annoying for residents, but I have had a sound meter at the front of that cave, and there is no way the noise of the music would carry a long way.

"We face the system into the cave to prevent the noise carrying out, and it would be hard for it to penetrate 30ft of rock," he said.

He was not sure whether any more parties would be held if they were going to be invaded by uninvited people who were causing bad feeling.

Another partygoer told the Gazette reports of people being "drugged out of their eyeballs" were exaggerated.

"The residents could have been confusing people being tired for drugs. If you've been up all night at a party, you don't look that good by 6am the next morning."

He said he had been to several parties with no trouble, but violence had erupted one Sunday morning three weeks ago.

"It was around 6am when I saw a group of lads fighting with baseball bats - I heard later they were from Millom," he said.

However police have repeated safety warnings after a diver drowned at Hodge Close on Sunday. Thirty-year-old David Arthur Evans, an experienced diver from the Sherrington area of Wigan, failed to surface after a dive.

His body was recovered from the floor of the waterlogged cave by a sub-aqua team from Yorkshire who were visiting the deep water cave, a popular haunt for divers.

Members of the sub-aqua team, which included a doctor, tried unsuccessfully to revive him.

Hodge Close Quarry has claimed the lives of many experienced divers over the past few years, said Chief Insp John Gloag of Barrow police.

He said it showed how dangerous the quarry area could be as a site for parties. He added: "It is somewhat ironic that a week after we had a major illegal party there, that unfortunately this gentleman has come to grief in a waterlogged quarry area.

Land agents Smith-Gore said they still planned to blow up the entrances to the caverns to stop the parties.

Mr Gordon Windle said access to the caverns was gained by tunnels which would be blocked by blowing up the entrances.

RAVE CAVES TO BE BLOWN

Caves at a Lake District beauty spot are to be blown up in a drastic bid to prevent them being used for illegal acid house parties.

More than a thousand people attended the latest "cave rave" on Saturday night, but police say the parties should be stopped soon before someone is killed.

Nearby residents also want a stop put to the raves. They say hundreds of youngsters wander around "drugged out of their brains", use their gardens as toilets, and keep them awake all night with loud music and the constant stream of traffic.

Youngsters travel from all over the country to the parties in the disused quarries at Hodge Close, Tilberthwaite, between Little Langdale and Coniston. Residents say they take place every fortnight and seem to be a well-organised business venture.

Now land agents for Lord Egremont, whose estate encompasses the site, say they will blow up the caves to prevent a fatal accident and stop the parties.

More than a thousand people descended on Langdale on Saturday night and the early hours of Sunday.

Chief Insp John Gloag, of Barrow police, says he had a team of men turning cars away from the area, and a generator was also confiscated.

He said the parties were illegal, because a public entertainments licence was needed as music was being provided and a charge being made.

Drugs were readily available at this kind of party, and people were trespassing, said Mr Gloag.

"One of our main concerns is for the safety of the party goers themselves. The terrain is dangerous, with disused quarries and mine workings, deep water, caves and ground that is riddled with caverns. It is only a matter of time before someone wandering about in the dark falls and kills themselves," said Mr Gloag.

He said small scale parties on the site had been going on for a number of years, but the situation now was getting "totally out of hand".

"Nearby residents have complained to us because they are having to clean up excreta, vomit and urine from their gardens, and the music and revving of car engines is keeping them awake.

— by —
Joanne Colley

Mr Gloag said only a small number of policemen had been turning cars away on Saturday was because ways into Hodge Close were limited. But he admitted that in the end, people were just parking their cars, and walking miles over the top of the fell to the venue.

He said police were planning to clamp down on the parties in the future.

"We are not against youngsters having fun. We are prepared to support pay parties, providing they are on a well organised site and licensed through the local authority, so the fire service can check safety aspects," he said.

Meanwhile, people living near the site say are fed up of the parties.

One lady, who asked not to be named because she was so frightened, said:

"People are wandering around drugged up to their eyeballs. The parties are happening every fortnight, and more and more people come. We knew police were going to be in the area, so we packed our young children off to their grandmothers. There is one hell of a noise of night until lunch time day, and there is rubbish litter all over the place.

Party goers have knocked on her door to use her toilet and damaged her car parked.

On opening her door morning, she had packet of drugs doorstep, she said.

"It has got to the where everybody is frightened to go out. She said the event well organised and heard charges of £ and £40 were made.

Malcolm Grindrod, member of Langdale and Mountain Rescue Team, he was very concerned the parties.

"I have seen parties ping children off and they should be warned dangers.

"There are drops, crags and caves. I the body of a person fallen and died in area from a 40ft drop and I wouldn't let my there because it's not Mr Grindrod.

Another lady who to be named said she frightened."

Lord orders all-night party cave 'blown-up'

Fatality fears as 1,000 walk over fell tops

By BILL MYERS

A CONISTON cave used for illegal all-night 'rave' parties by up to 1,000 people is to be dynamited to prevent danger to partygoers and disturbance for residents.

The industrial relic left by quarrying at Hodge Close, Tilberthwaite, will be blown up on behalf of owner Lord Egremont.

His land agents said the action was being taken to prevent the parties and stop potentially-fatal accidents.

It comes after a long series of parties, the latest being last Saturday night when up to 1,000 people arrived from all over the country.

Police did their best to turn away cars from reaching the illegal party, but drivers just parked further away and walked to the quarries over fell tops.

NOISY

A police spokesman said partygoers were putting themselves at risk in an area riddled with caverns and deep ponds.

'It is only a matter of time before someone wandering about in the dark falls and kills themselves,' he said.

Police have been inundated with complaints from residents, who have to put up with the noise of engines revving at night almost every fortnight.

One woman claimed: 'There is one hell of a noise of traffic all night until lunchtime on Sunday.'

The partygoers also left litter everywhere and used gardens as public toilets.

Quarry 'event is put back

By Chris Hill

PLANS for a second open-air house 'rave' in Barrow, just two weeks after the first, have been put off.

Raindance, London-based party promoter, was planning to apply to Barrow Council to hold a party for thousands of people on August 31, a fortnight after Nemisis holds its party for 6,000 at Roosecote sand quarry on August 17.

But now Raindance has decided to hold off on its application and try to set up the 'rave' in September, leaving a longer gap between the two.

Kirk Field, of Raindance, said the organisation is on tour parties in six venues around the country, and the work involved meant it did not have time to devote to the Barrow party.

MORE NEWS ★ MORE

O WELCOME IN HESE HILLSIDES

STAR REPORTER

ENTY hippies rrested yesterday ,000 "New Age llers" tried to a music festival in

But furious locals said the defiant hippies had already "vandalised land".

tanley of his illed b the tra oursuin the un

ARE N UP

ve been about six r and they seem g worse. You don't g to bed because you won't get any

rightened to go out. this Saturday be- le were shouting e house. We have car and we daren't n the road, because ple driving to the as high as kites,"

on Windle, consul- agents Smith Gore, ion had been taken the caves to stop arties.

ery concerned that going to be killed. eld meetings with roups that use the s divers, abseilers, motorcyclists, the rust and the Na- , and have agreed gns about trespass. s just getting too There are mines, hafts, caverns and are going to blow re, because that is t the party goers

also going to try the way to tres- d we are very con- t the use of drugs,"

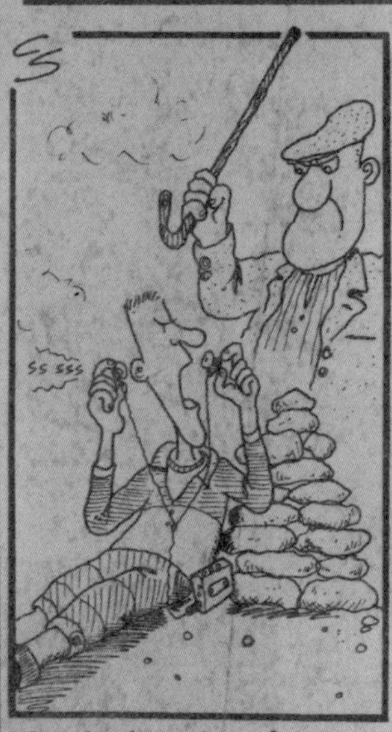

Shelbourn

"For the last time, I am not having an acid fell party!"

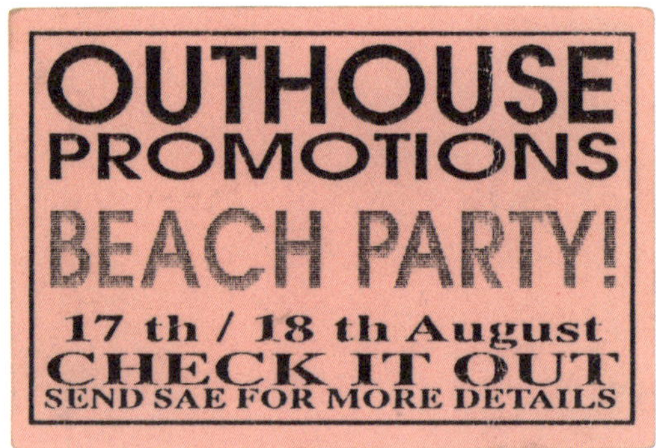

'I can tell you cracks about a particular night, which was the best one, 'cos there was another do on… a proper, fully-fledged, real do called Nemesis on the same night. I've got their flyer and ours… We were doing the promoting and some geezers came to my mate's house and said, "Look if you put the caves on tonight, then we'll come up there and we'll shoot you and take your gear." But, a lot of people came along to the caves anyway… We were going to do a beach party near there, a free one… well that's what we said, we just did it up at the caves.'

Extract from a conversation in relation to 'beach party' flyers distributed by Outhouse as a decoy for alleged rival promoters.

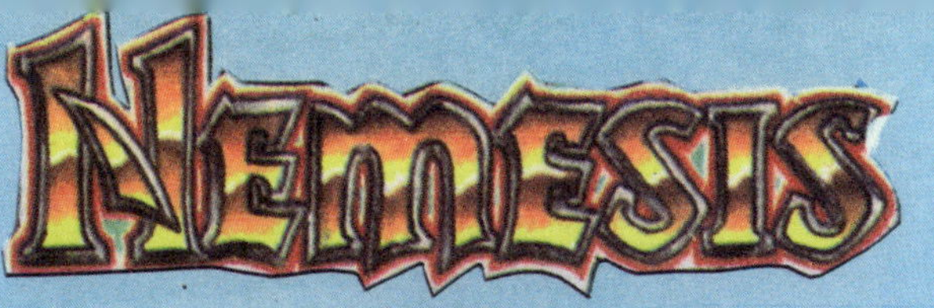

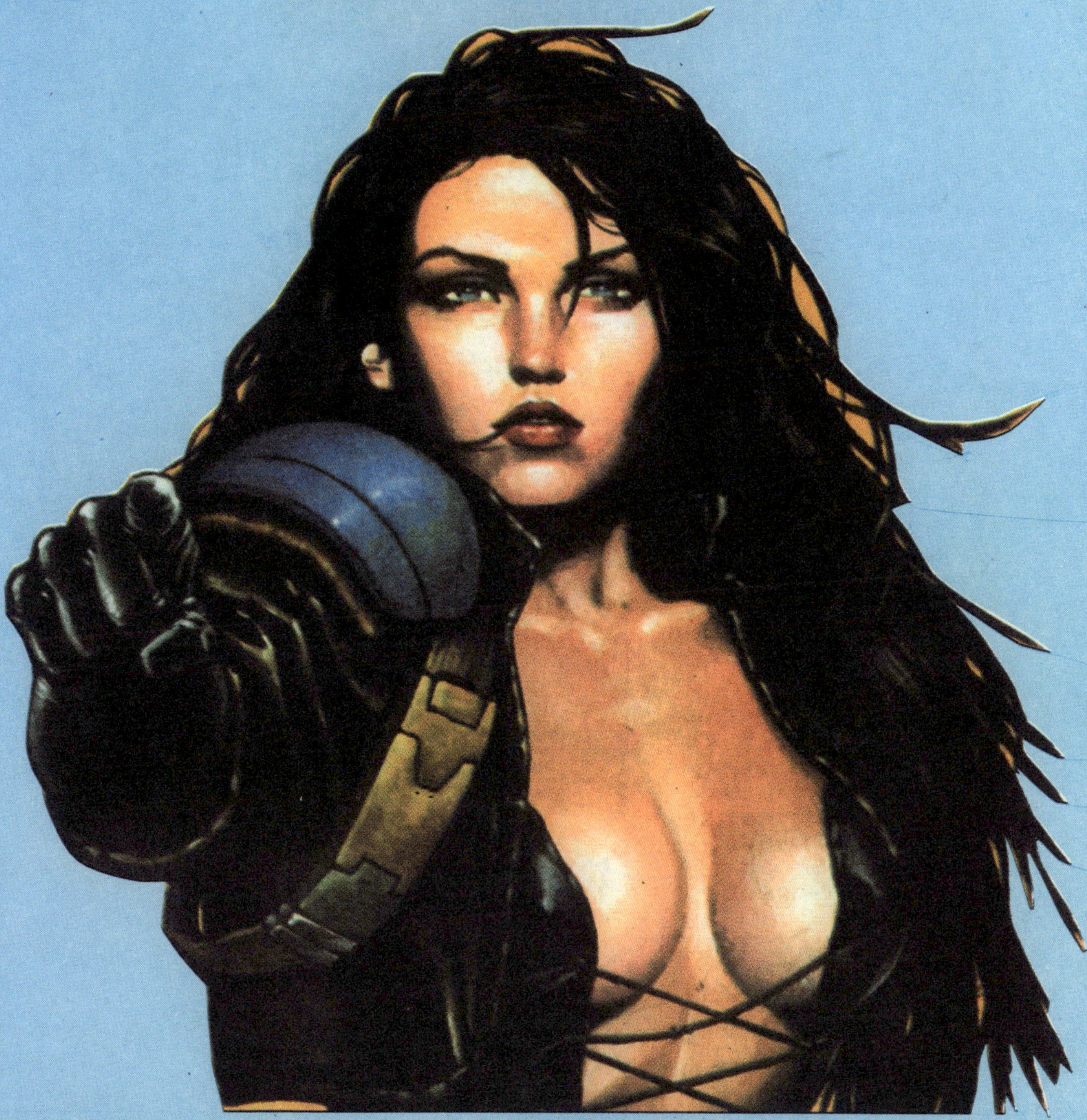

SATURDAY 17th AUGUST 1991

ALL NIGHT **8PM TO 8AM** ALL NIGHT

ROOSECOTE SAND QUARRY
BARROW IN FURNESS, CUMBRIA N/W

THIS IS AN **AMNESIA HOUSE** PROMOTION FOR
NEMESIS

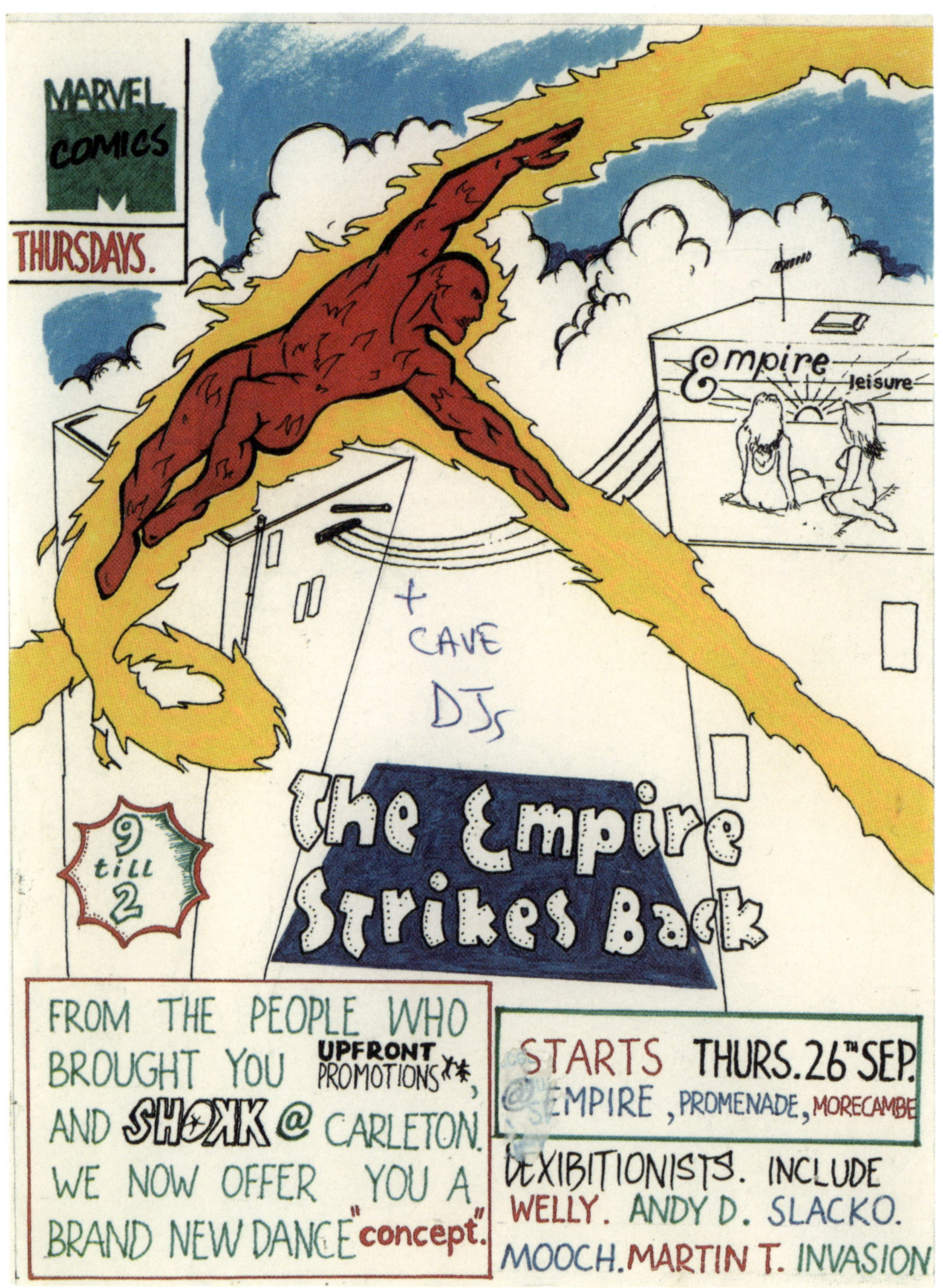

MARVEL
COMICS
M
THURSDAYS.
Empire leisure
+ CAVE DJs
9 till 2
the Empire Strikes Back
FROM THE PEOPLE WHO BROUGHT YOU UPFRONT PROMOTIONS **, AND SHOKK @ CARLETON. WE NOW OFFER YOU A BRAND NEW DANCE "concept".
STARTS THURS. 26TH SEP.
@ EMPIRE, PROMENADE, MORECAMBE
EXIBITIONISTS. INCLUDE WELLY. ANDY D. SLACKO. MOOCH. MARTIN T. INVASION

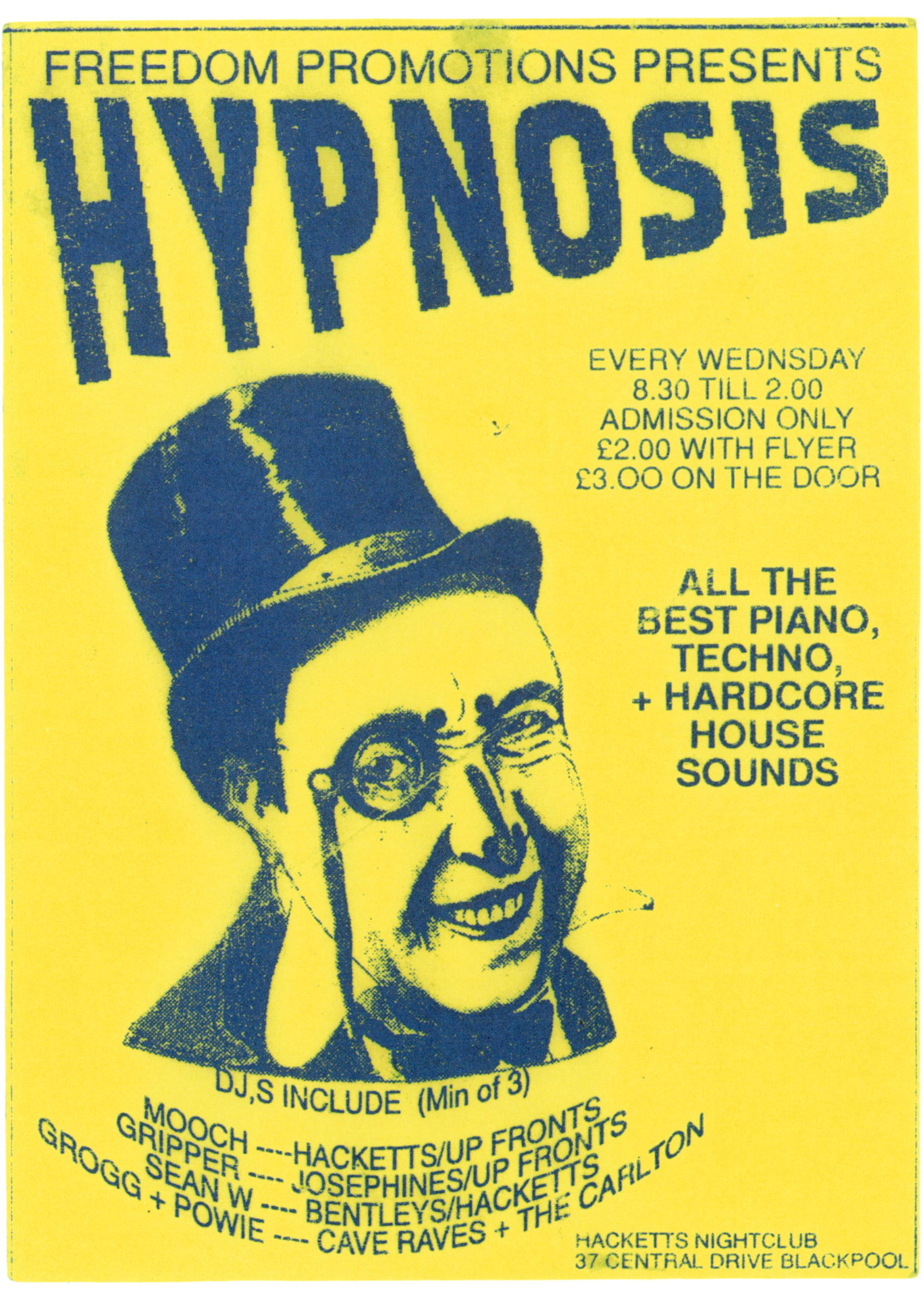
FREEDOM PROMOTIONS PRESENTS
HYPNOSIS
EVERY WEDNSDAY
8.30 TILL 2.00
ADMISSION ONLY
£2.00 WITH FLYER
£3.00 ON THE DOOR
ALL THE
BEST PIANO,
TECHNO,
+ HARDCORE
HOUSE
SOUNDS
DJ,S INCLUDE (Min of 3)
MOOCH ----HACKETTS/UP FRONTS
GRIPPER ---- JOSEPHINES/UP FRONTS
SEAN W ---- BENTLEYS/HACKETTS
GROGG + POWIE ---- CAVE RAVES + THE CARLTON
HACKETTS NIGHTCLUB
37 CENTRAL DRIVE BLACKPOOL

EVERY FORTNIGHT FROM FRIDAY 20TH SEPTEMBER

GRANGERS NIGHTCLUB, SAND LANE
WARTON, NR. CARNFORTH, LANCS.

DJs
THE CAVE CREW
POWIE
GROG
STEELY D

MC BUZZ

+

live PAs and special guest DJs

£2 members - £5 non-members
doors open 8.30 p.m. - be early

FREE MEMBERSHIP
available by sending s.a.e. to:
OUTHOUSE PROMOTIONS
the hollies, miller bridge,
ambleside, cumbria

Follow Carnforth A6. Turn at traffic lights.
Past train station for one mile then left in village.

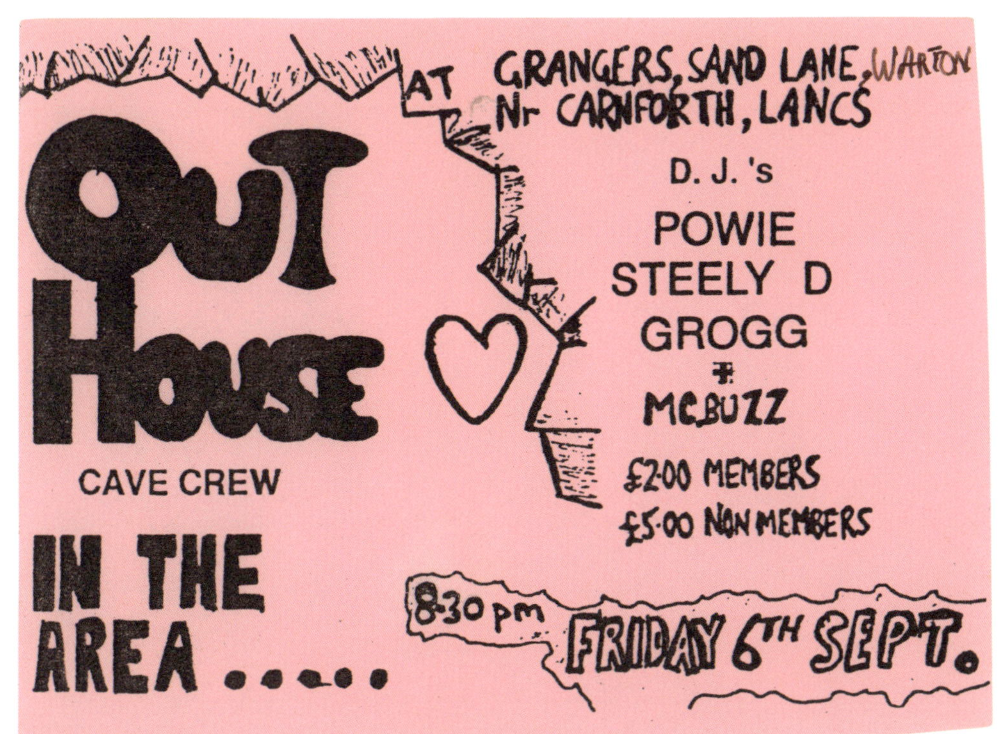

OUT HOUSE
CAVE CREW
IN THE AREA ......
AT GRANGERS, SAND LANE, WARTON
Nr CARNFORTH, LANCS
D.J.'s
POWIE
STEELY D
GROGG
+
MC BUZZ
£2·00 MEMBERS
£5·00 NON MEMBERS
8·30 pm
FRIDAY 6th SEPT.

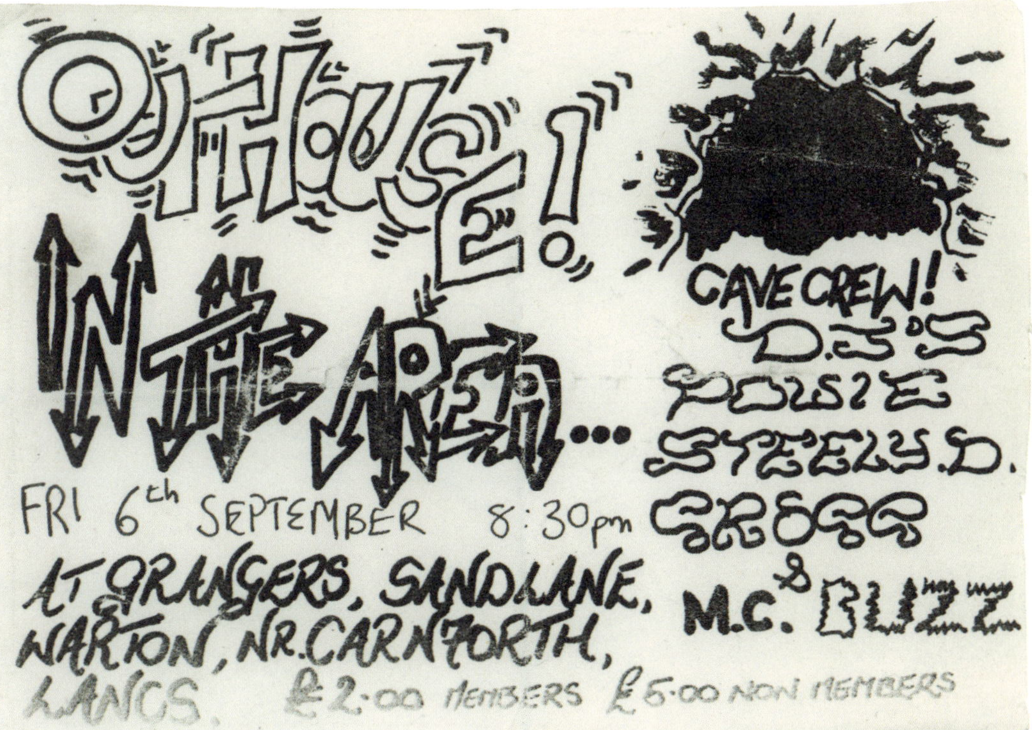

OUTHOUSE!
IN THE AREA...
CAVE CREW!
D.J's
POWIE
STEELY D.
GROGG
M.C. BUZZ
FRI 6th SEPTEMBER 8:30pm
AT GRANGERS, SAND LANE,
WARTON, NR. CARNFORTH,
LANCS. £2·00 MEMBERS £5·00 NON MEMBERS

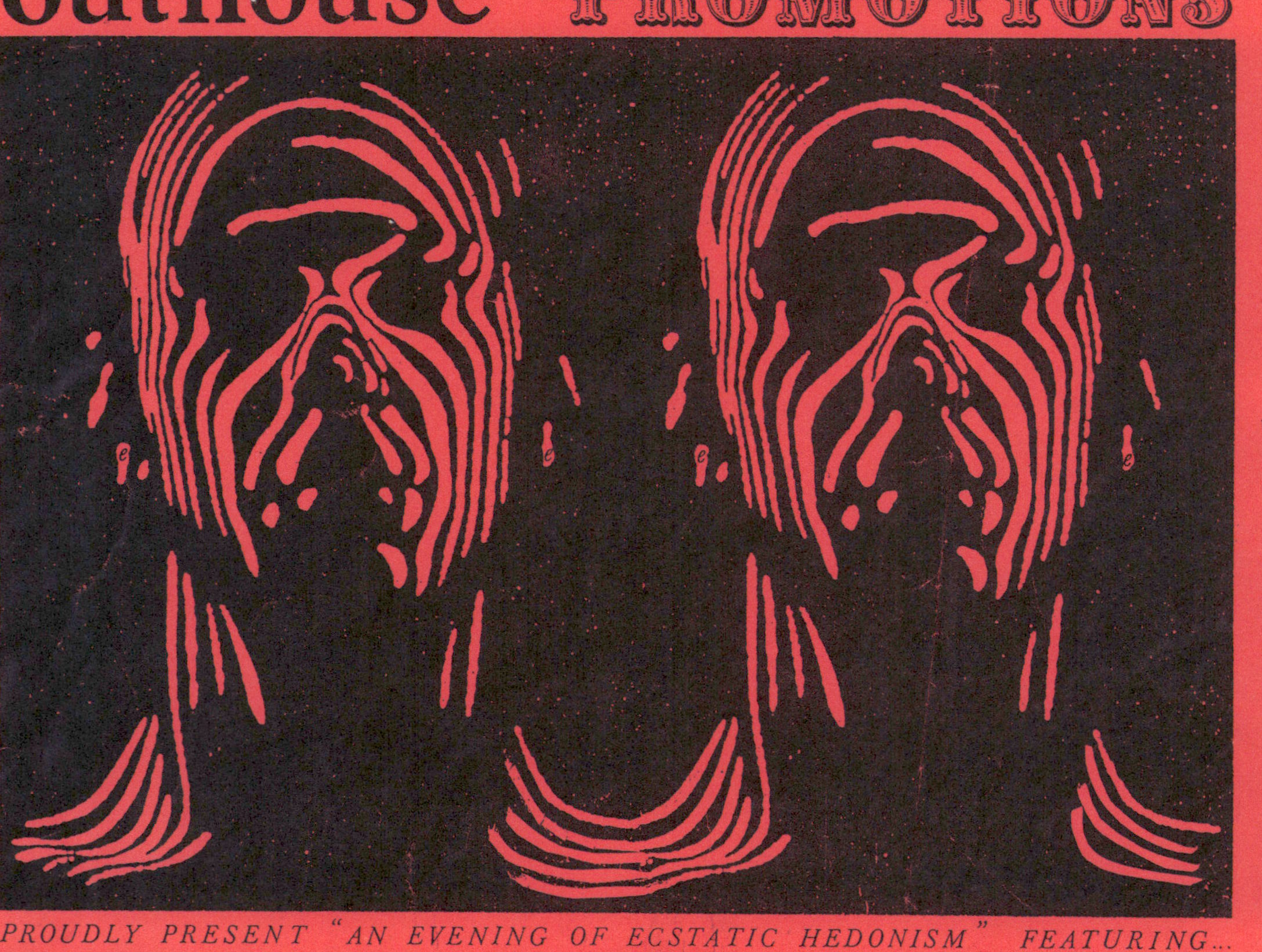

outhouse PROMOTIONS
IMAGES NIGHTCLUB
mangreyn
FRIDAY 11 OCTOBER
PROUDLY PRESENT "AN EVENING OF ECSTATIC HEDONISM" FEATURING...
THE SLAVE CREW

RAVE

11th Oct   11th Oct

THE CAVE CREW

FEATURING DJs

POWIE, STEELY D, GROGG

(THE BEST IN THE NORTH WEST)

AT

IMAGES NIGHTCLUB

LAYGATE ROUNDABOUT, SOUTH SHIELDS

(NEAREST METRO CHICHESTER)

ADMISSION £5 ON DOOR

TICKETS NOW ON SALE £5 BEHIND BAR

8.00 TILL 2.00

NO DRESS RESTRICTION

TATTOOS AND WIGS WELCOME

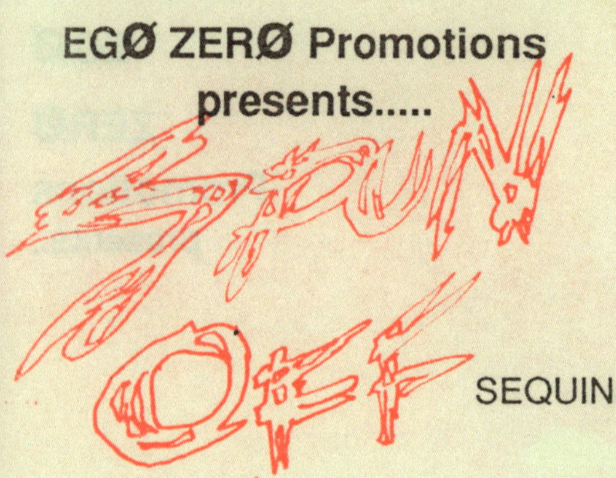

EGØ ZERØ Promotions
presents.....

The Hardcore, Techno &
Piano, House Night
All the Best Tunes laid down by the area
top DJ's **THE HYPE DJ'S**
SEQUINS (BLACKPOOL), 5TH AVENUE (MANCHESTER)
UPHORIA.

THE CAVE CREW

DJ GROGG + DJ POWIE

**THE CAVES, HACKETTS (BLACKPOOL)
HYPNOSIS, THE CARLTON (MORECAMBE)**

ATTRACTIONS...

**MASSIVE PROJECTION SCREEN OVER DANCE FLOOR
SHOWING INCREDIBLE PROJECTIONS AND
MANIC VIDEOS
+LASER DISCS ALL NIGHT**
Chill-Out Areas (with ice pops on sale)
3K Sound System and Amazing Visuals

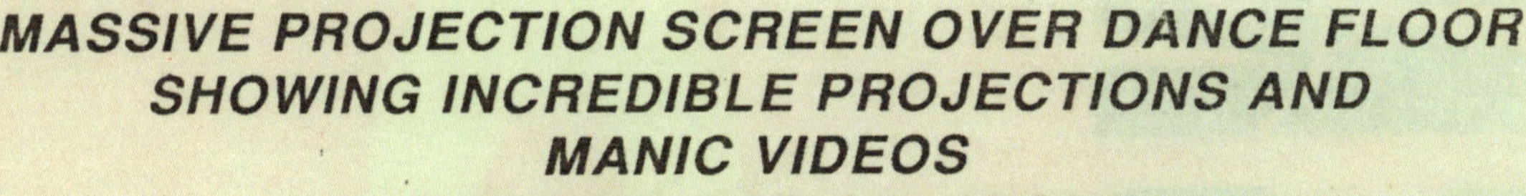

Admission **only £3.50** on the door.
B U F F E R S   N I G H T C L U B (ULVERSTON)
FOLLOW SIGNS FOR THE TRAIN STATION (**It's on the train station**)
8.45 pm till LATE

<u>BE **EARLY!**</u>
These flyers are available in <u>four colours</u>. Collect all four and get in
FREE!!!

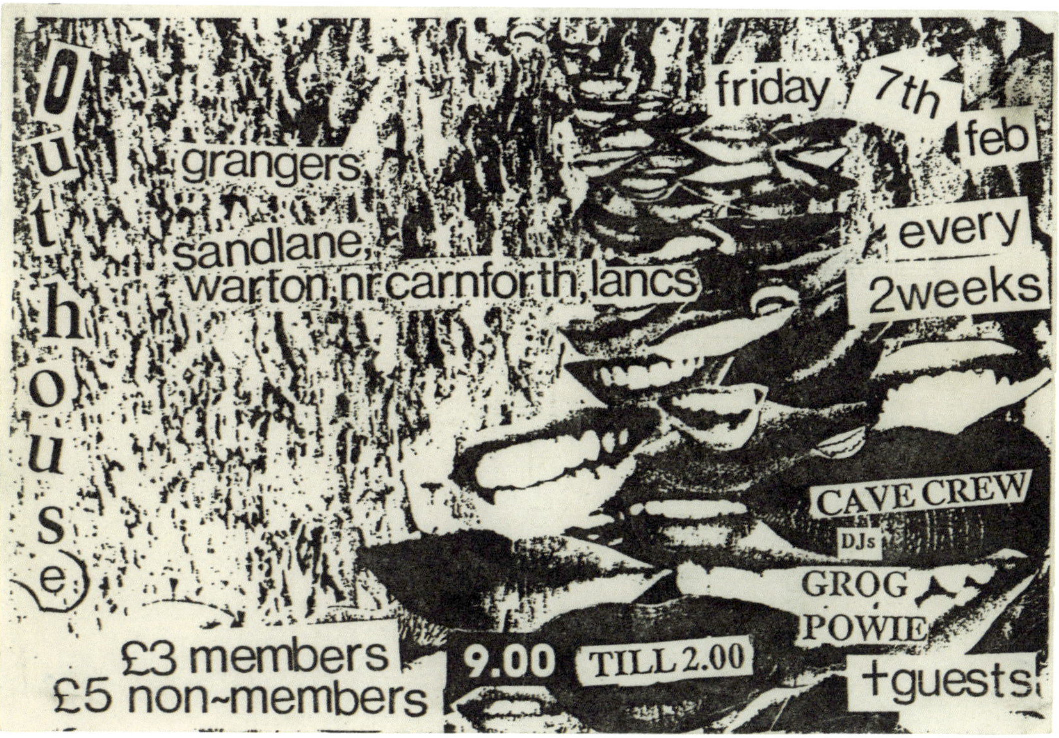

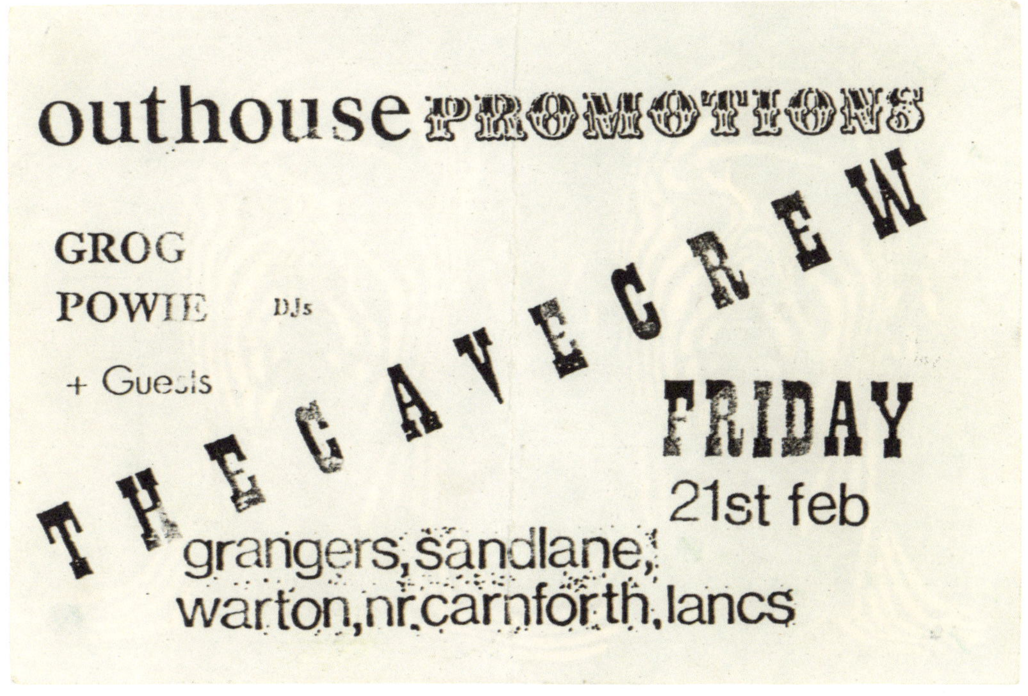

Outhouse
grangers
sandlane,
warton, nr. carnforth, lancs
friday 7th feb
every 2 weeks
CAVE CREW
DJs
GROG
POWIE
£3 members
£5 non-members
9.00 TILL 2.00
+guests

outhouse PROMOTIONS
GROG
POWIE DJs
+ Guests
THECAVECREW
FRIDAY
21st feb
grangers, sandlane,
warton, nr. carnforth, lancs

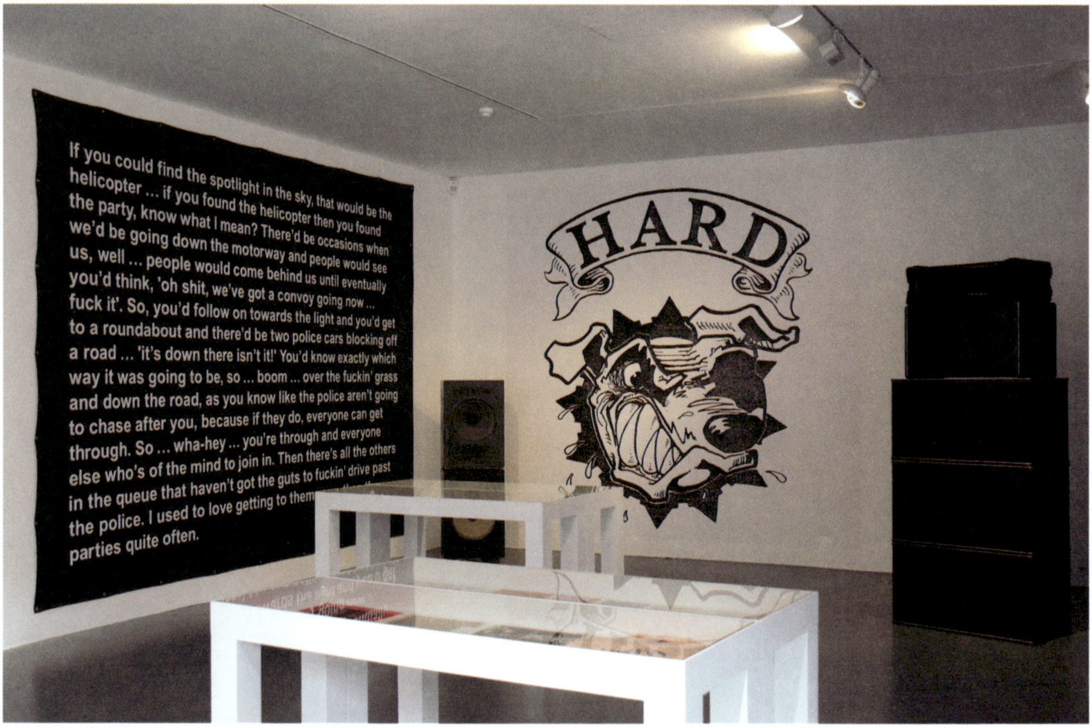

Installation detail of **Real Arcadia** at Temple Bar Gallery, Dublin. 2007.

Reconstruction of the speaker stacks used by the Cave Crew, and sketch by Steely D.

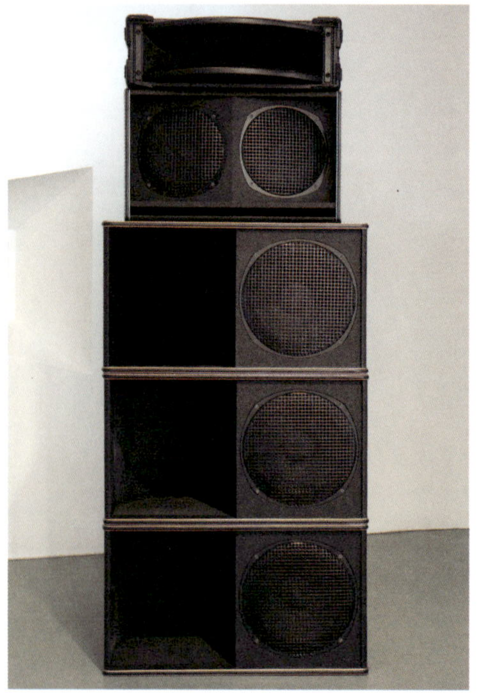

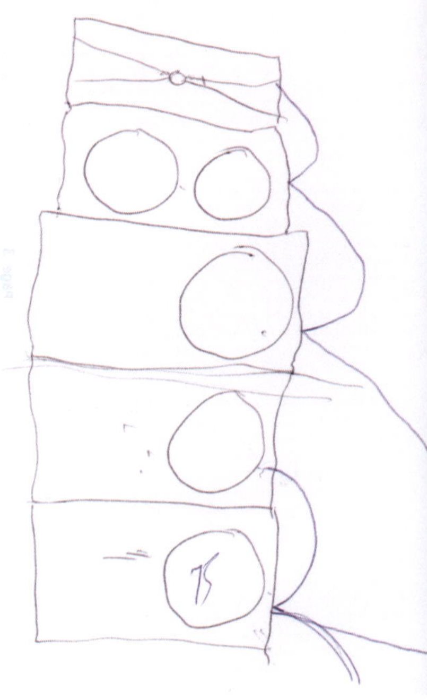

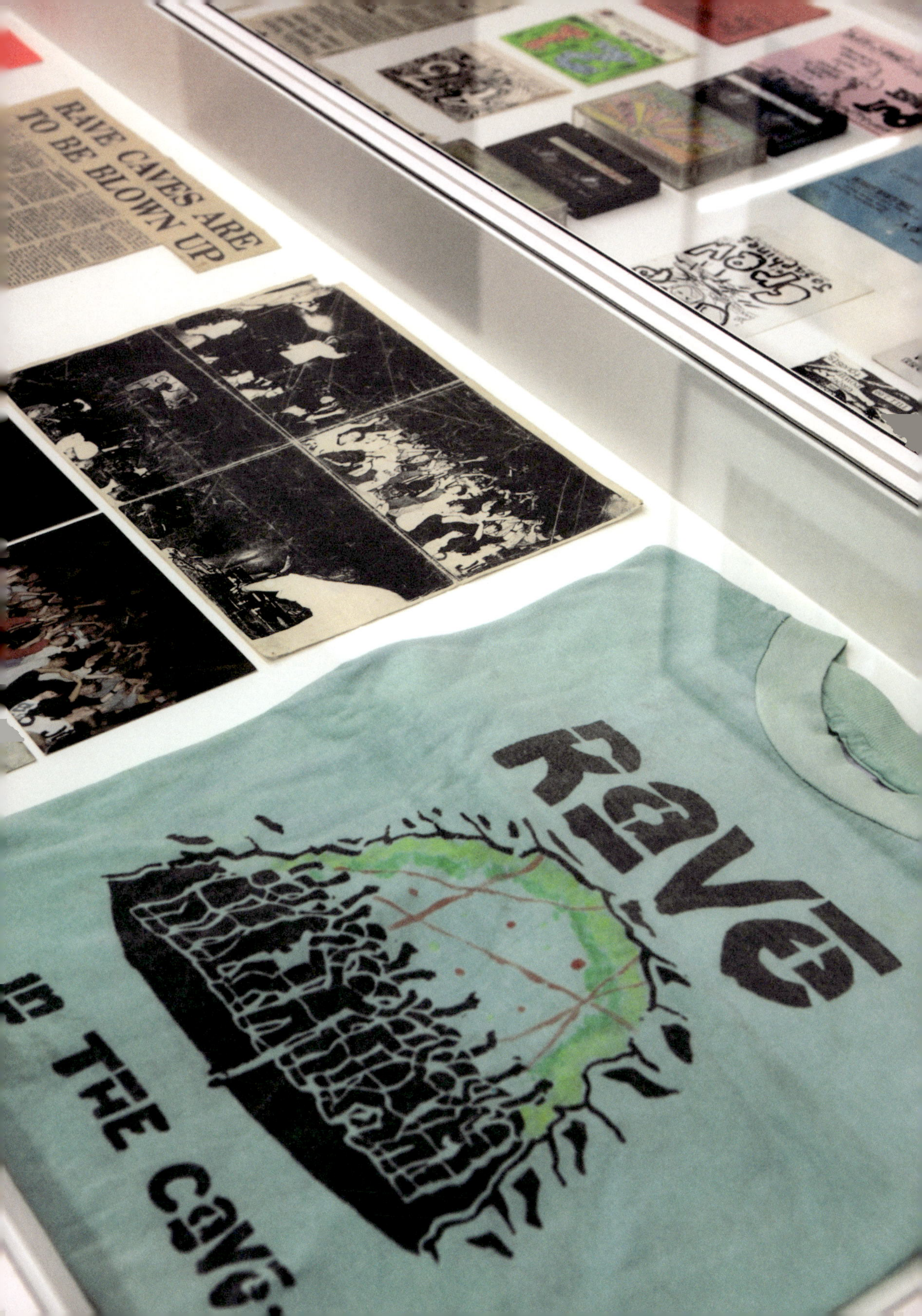

RAVE CAVES ARE
TO BE BLOWN UP
RAVE
IN THE CAVE

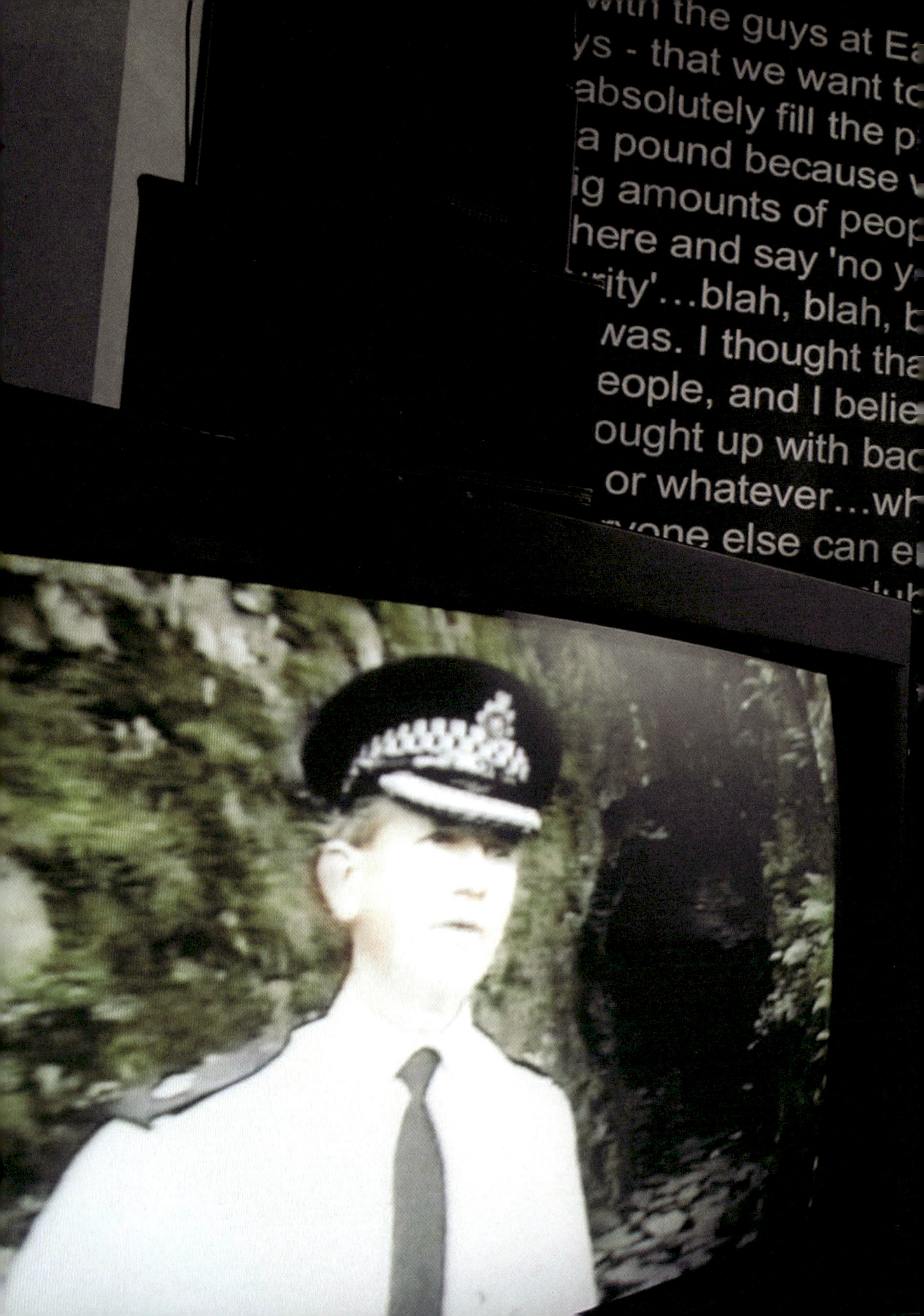
with the guys at Ea
ys - that we want to
absolutely fill the p
a pound because
g amounts of peop
here and say 'no y
rity'…blah, blah, b
was. I thought tha
eople, and I belie
ought up with ba
or whatever…wh
one else can e

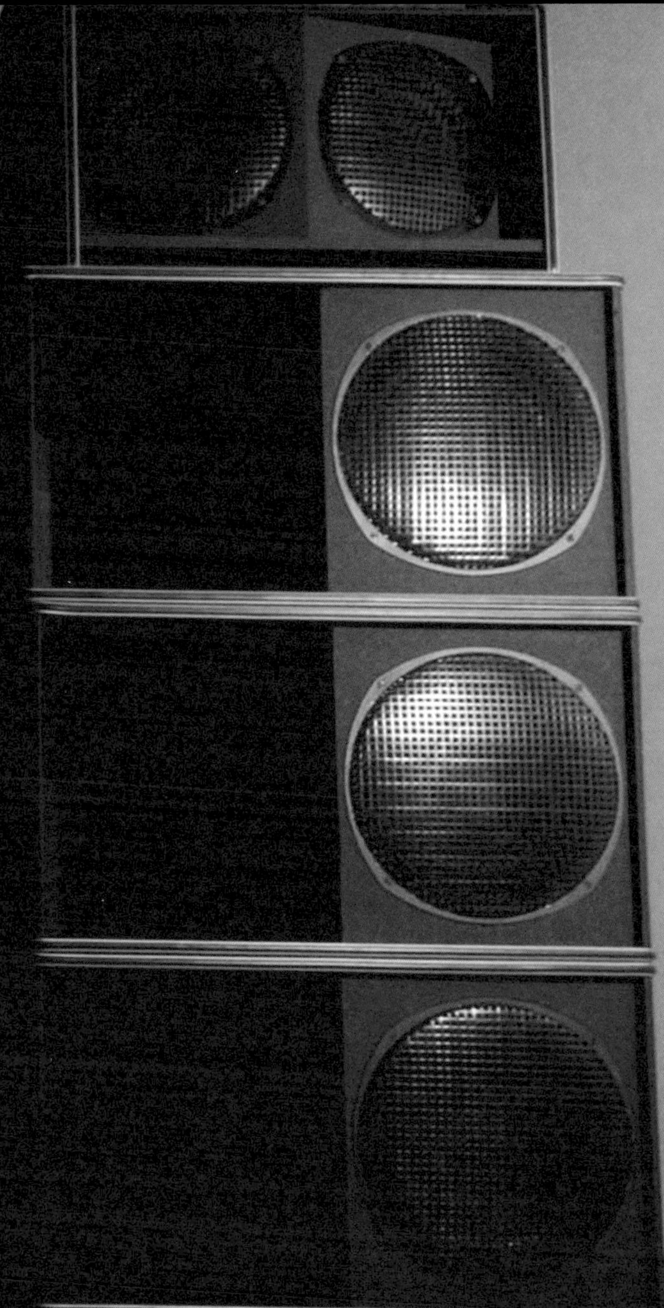

Installation detail of **Real Arcadia** at BALTIC Centre for Contemporary Art, Gateshead. 2006.

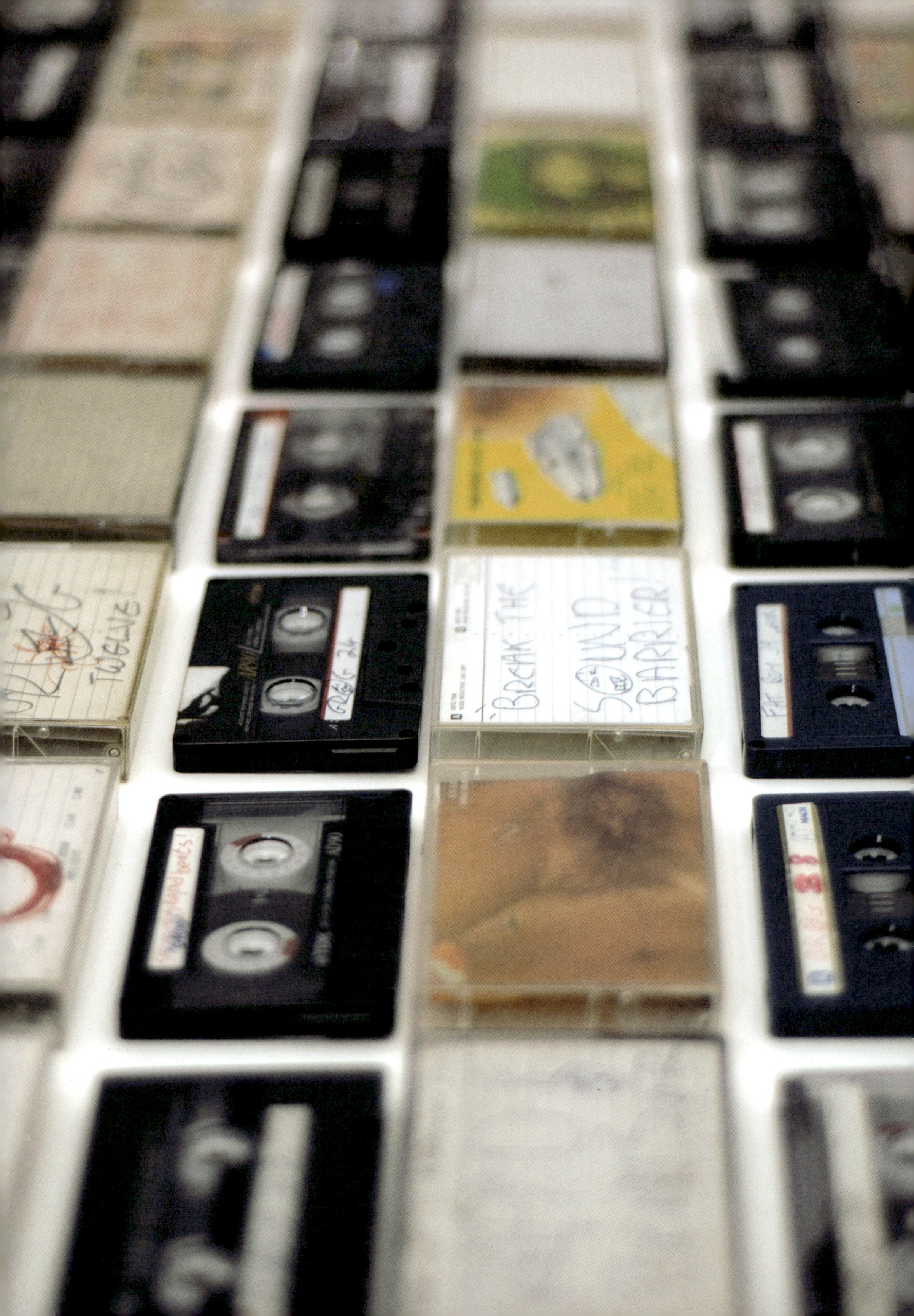

TWELVE!
GREG 24
BREAK THE
SOUND
BARRIER!

Sacred Selections

Sacred Selections
A series of pipe organ recitals featuring experimental transcriptions
of underground music (Northern Soul, Happy Hardcore and Black Metal),
posters and handbills
2005 – ongoing

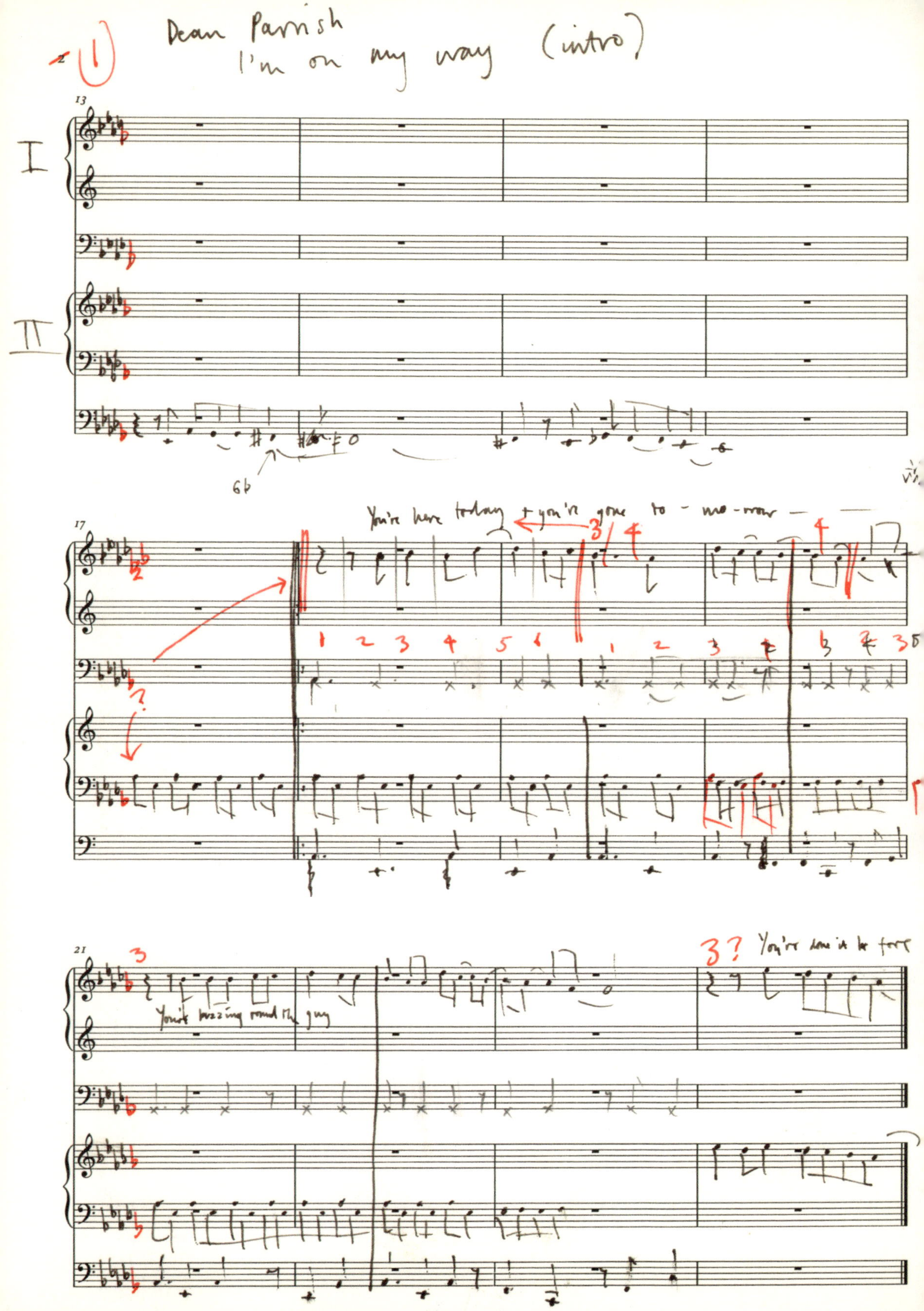
Dean Parrish
I'm on my way (intro)
You're here today + you're gone to - mo - rrow
You're buzzing round the guy
You're done it be fore

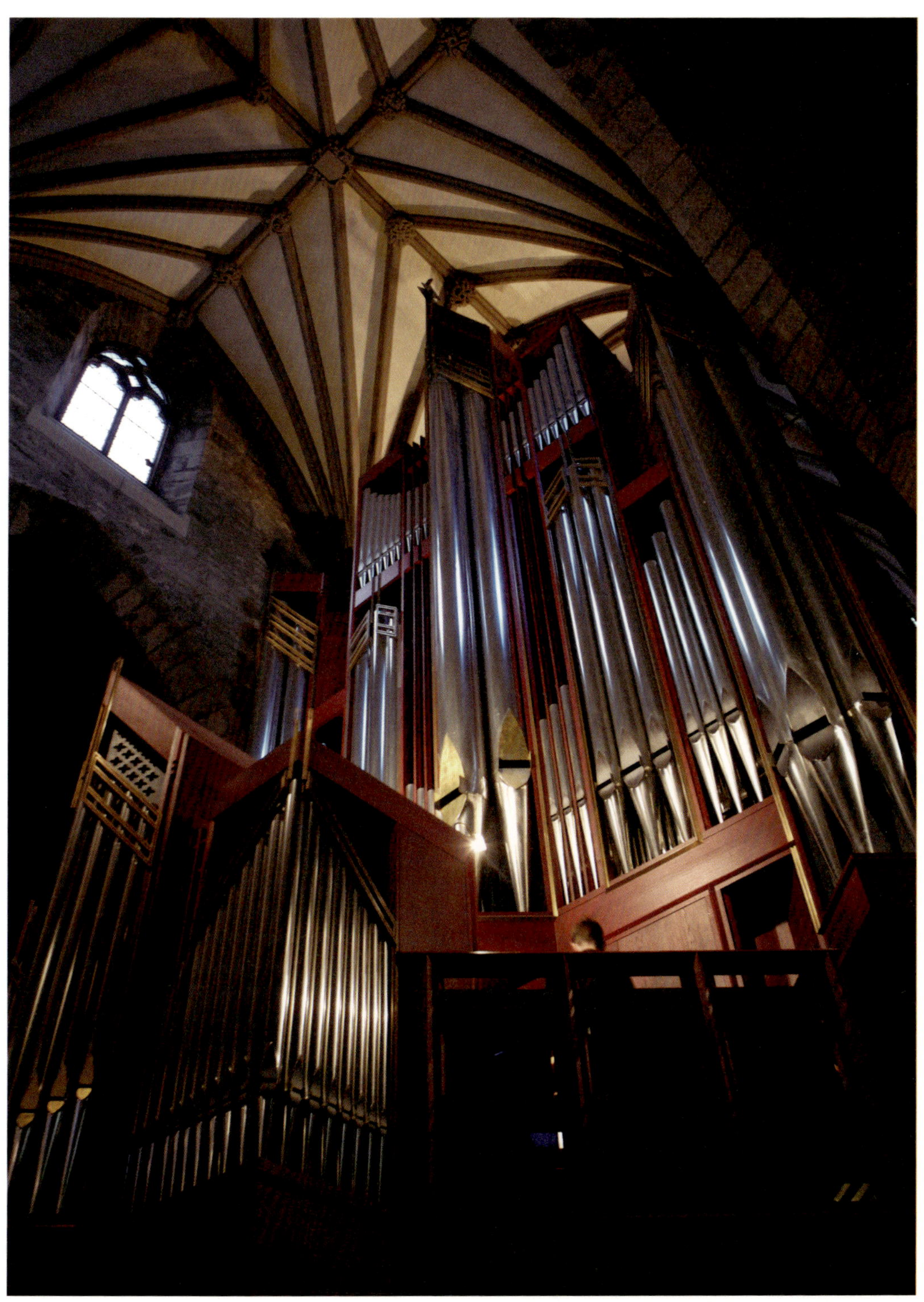

Performance at St Giles' Cathedral, Edinburgh. 24 August 2006.

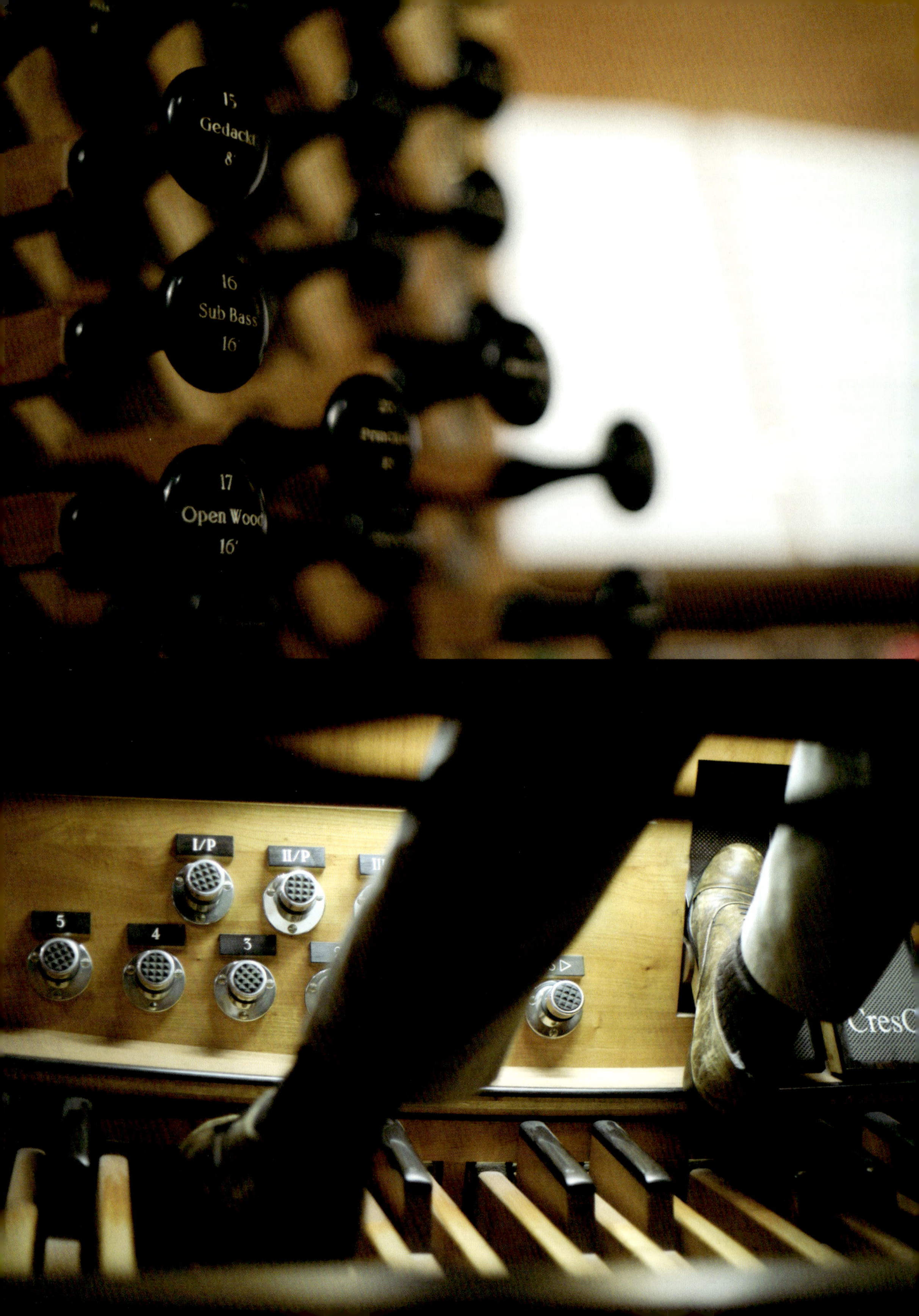

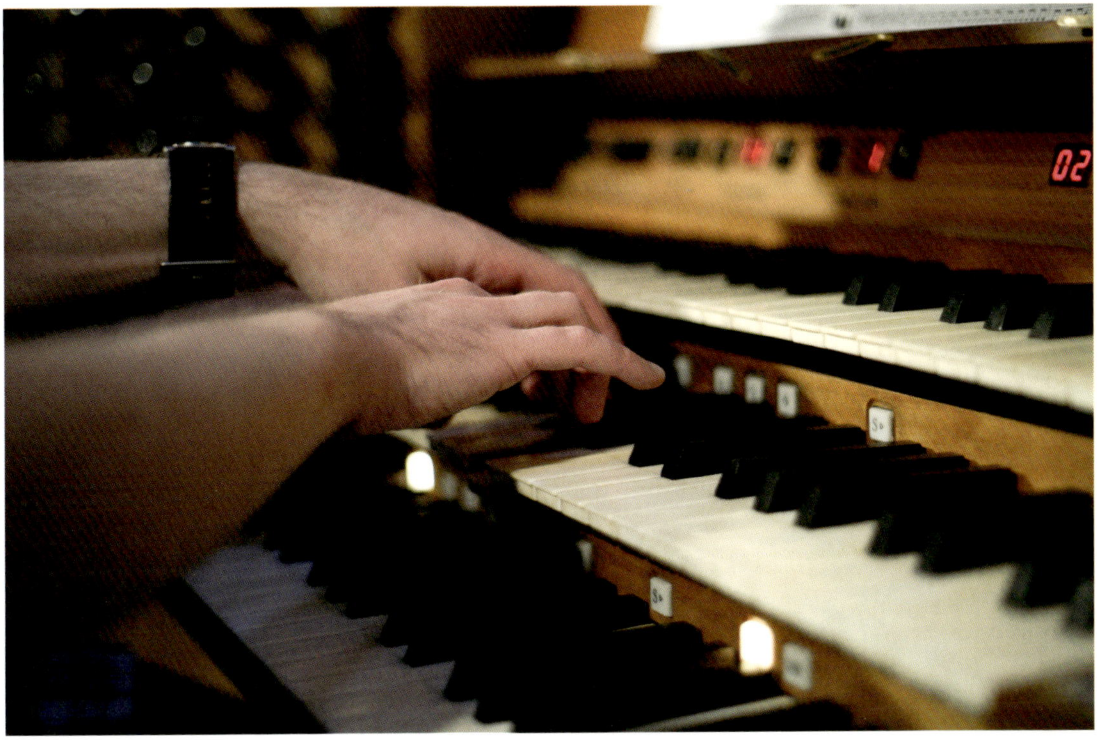

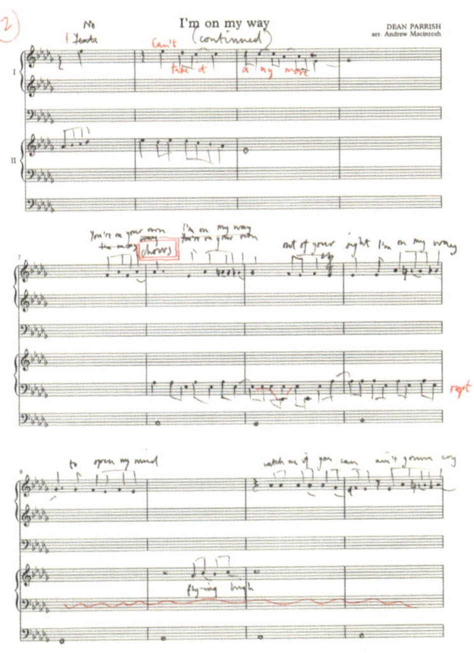

I'm on my way
(continued)
DEAN PARRISH
arr. Andrew Macintosh

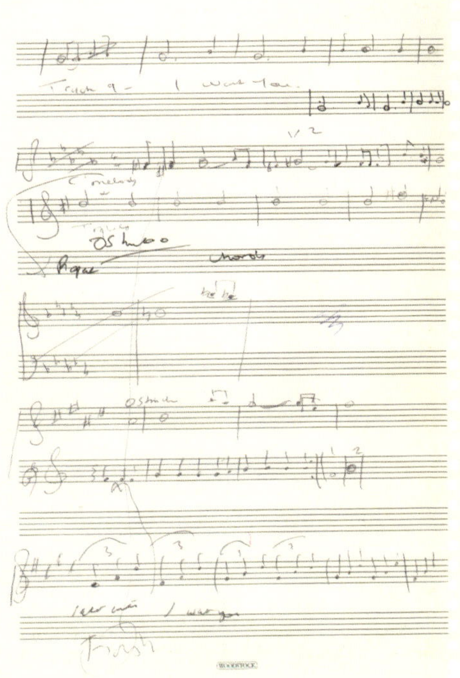

Passion and Ecstasy of a Tokyo Train Driver

Momus

Three years ago I was riding a suburban Tokyo train belonging to the Tokyu Company. My journey, which was entirely above ground, took me from Okayama to Meguro, from the outer suburbs of the world's largest city to the centre.

I was standing in the first carriage, right behind the driver. As we passed traffic crossings and an endless succession of tidy clapboard houses, I began to notice a series of odd cries, muffled by glass.

The cries were coming from the white-gloved driver himself. Alone in his cabin, he was accompanying his actions with staccato shouts. It was astonishing; yet weirdly, I was the only passenger paying any attention.

My first thought was that the driver was mentally ill. I had to admire the train company's lack of prejudice in giving such a responsible job to someone with Tourette's Syndrome, but couldn't help worrying for our safety.

And yet, the man did seem exceptionally well focused. At each station he made an immaculate white-gloved gesture – a series of florid manual curlicues more like the motions of an orchestral conductor than a train driver.

Pointing at the TV screens on his console showing the doors, the driver pulled the train out of each station with both hands on his accelerator lever, uttering as if by compulsion his ecstatic falling cry: 'Kkkkyyyyyooooooooo!' Crossing points or passing other trains, he made similar noises. They seemed less like words than explosions of passion for the regular events of the job – a passion as formalised as the whoops and howls of Kabuki actors.

More speculations rattled through my mind. Was this a trainee driver, taught to call out loud the actions he was making in the same way that, as a Learner Driver in Britain, I had been taught to say 'Mirror, Signal, Manoeuvre'? I began to see, beside the driver in the cabin, the contours of a spectral guru driver appear: a calm, modest yet deeply authoritative Master of the Train.

This trainee driver, I speculated, was addressing his ghost, his internalised train master, and calling out with passionate capitulation a rote roll-call of his duties for the master to hear and approve.

Later, a Japanese friend told me that this behaviour is common and normal in Japan. All train drivers shout out their actions in this way, not just trainees.

I realised that, brought up in the West, I'd been educated to think of a train driver as, on the one hand, a robot, a servant, and, on the other, as 'an individual who just happens, at this moment, to be driving a train, but could be so much more than that if he wanted to be. So don't box him in!'

Western society covers its hierarchical verticality with the cant of 'equality of opportunity' (which of course entails its less benign cousin, inequality of result). Sure, the President is above you, but you too could be president one day!

Japanese society – in principle, at least – is super-flat, distributed. Ultimate value might fall at any point on the horizontal plane. Everybody is as important as everybody else; everybody bows to everybody else. The capitulation is mutual, the investment total.

The West prefers us to be divided, to wear masks, to adopt a casual, pragmatic, rather non-committal attitude to our jobs. Only selected people (the entrepreneur, the artist, the musician, the sexual pervert) are really seen as vocational in a passionate way, the way that would make you say, 'He's what he does right to his core, he lives it 24 hours a day.'

A Western train driver might make us feel indifference, scorn or pity. He might make us hope he had a nice family and hobbies to compensate for the under-rewarded, uninteresting drudgery of his job. But this Tokyu Line employee seemed to be a train driver from his peaked cap down to his boots and all the way through to his very soul. He had made train driving his religion.

I was lost in admiration and jealousy. I wanted this man's commitment, his dignity. Not necessarily to train driving – to anything, really. I wanted to wear white gloves and make delicate ceremonial gestures even while doing something completely pragmatic and down-to-earth. I wanted to cry out with ecstasy every time I crossed points, or cooked ramen.

As this driver, I speculated, I would never feel unimportant. I would feel, in fact, like a star. An everyday star. I would catch glimpses of fascination and envy from children and adults alike. I'd never be surprised to find myself being photographed or filmed. It would seem perfectly natural that video game arcades should feature simulations of my job, or artworks recreate my place of work, recast as the ideal public space.

My glamour would be apparent, though lightly worn. At the end of my shift I'd hand over to the next driver with a low bow and a deep sense of satisfaction. Not the satisfaction of having an onerous job behind me and quality time ahead, but a sense of deep joy that I had the same professional glories ahead of me tomorrow, and forever.

Whatever I was paid would be okay. My reward would be a deep sense of legitimacy. Superlegitimacy, a rich reward.

Although this only looked like train driving, in fact it was something tremendously Japanese; a sense of almost fanatical dedication, a fulfilment of self in a social role, an internalisation of societal requirement, a going-to-extremes, an etiquette, a sense of honour.

I was reminded of how Mishima's father, reluctant to see his son become something so undignified as a writer, had said, 'Very well, if you become a writer, at least become Japan's best.' (Mishima proceeded to do just that).

The ecstasy of my train driver seemed to confirm something very important. Namely, that happiness does not lie in avoiding or escaping your social role, but in embracing it completely and joyfully.

Stop trying to deny the social category you're in! Relax into your role, or, rather, stiffen into it (in all senses). The clarity will help everyone! By limiting yourself, you will set yourself free. By concentrating on what's here and now and practical, you can reach the eternal and the mysterious. The sublime is something you can organise.

I thought again about superlegitimacy when I first saw the work of Matt Stokes. By organising a Northern Soul night as if it were an early Christian ceremony, transcribing Happy Hardcore and Black Metal anthems for the organ, and reconstructing a sound system used at illegal raves, Stokes seemed to be conferring on volatile, evanescent or underground events some kind of retrospective legitimacy.

Neither far enough away from us to be safely designated as 'history' nor close enough to be part of our deceptively familiar daily habits, the kind of events he chose to commemorate loomed in some uncanny valley, some uncomfortable purgatory, some between place.

The legitimacy Stokes' projects have recognised and celebrated could be seen as 'superlegitimacy' because of the utter dedication of the participants.

Like my Tokyo train driver, the 'Soulies', 'Metallers', club promoters, church organists, pipe organ builders, or the organisers of cave parties, believed utterly in what they were doing. Their motivations were not principally financial, nor were they solely interested in dividing themselves or detaching themselves in order to get reluctantly through the day, and through their lives. These were vocational and euphoric projects, animated by the devotion of otakus and acolytes.

By their gestures, their total dedication, their discovery of an otherness in the everyday, their logistical participation in something collective, these people communicated a controlled ecstasy as enviable as my train driver's.

To commemorate ephemeral rituals years later was to assert, as I did of the train driver, that social value could fall at any point on society's horizontal plane. Religion need not be hierarchical, with rites sanctioned high up in a church bureaucracy then distributed through a network of religious functionaries scattered throughout the world. New rites – perfectly legitimate ones – can arise anywhere, quite spontaneously.

These new rites might well emerge from subcultures, because, in a system that's horizontal and 'superflat', a subculture is no less legitimate than an elite. In fact, because of the loyalty of its acolytes, and their refusal to divide themselves or hold back from an ecstatic immersion in an entirely pragmatic sublime, a subculture might be a more legitimate site for the emergence of new rites – and a new sense of what's ultimately 'right' – than more official sources.

Kafka tells the story of how panthers broke into the temple, disturbing the holy ritual by drinking the ceremonial wine. They did this year after year, at exactly the same moment. Eventually it was integrated into the ceremony.

I wonder if my train driver has a wife? If he does, I'd like to imagine her referring to him as 'Mr Train Driver' in bed. I imagine him wearing his uniform even on days when he has no work, wrapped up in the honour and freedom of what we'd see as a categorical limitation. I imagine my train driver hero walking by the sea, and even the sea calling out a cheerful greeting: 'Thank you for your great work! Otsukare samadeshita!'

Superlegitimacy is the opposite of anomie, and it's beyond price. You can find it in subculture or above ground, in daylight, right there in the middle of the working day. It's the process by which meaning is produced.

Music often accompanies a sense of superlegitimacy. Real or imagined music. Tender, lovely music plays in Japan when a train enters a station, the tinkling arpeggios of an electronic music box. The arriving train is 'the beloved', and even commuters, whose relationship with it is purely instrumental, for a moment feel like otaku, train fanatics, when they hear this music. They sense the deep legitimacy, the profound charisma, of the arriving train and the team who are deeply privileged to operate it.

Just as anomie is a vicious circle (we hate the trains, so we trash them, so they become even more dismal, and we hate and trash them more), so superlegitimacy is a virtuous one, an upward spiral. We love this, we improve this, we improve ourselves, we make something out of nothing, and out of fleeting events we form lasting relationships.

Genuine joy and passion – no matter how ragged, renegade or subcultural they may at first appear – cannot help but become superlegitimate in the end. All you need is repetition... and an archaeologist of the recent past who's observant and respectful enough to isolate and identify new forms of holiness as they arrive.

Sacred Selections, one of four readings.

'Somewhere out in that black dim night gloom – in this city of
what looked like perpetual night – there was an oasis known as
the Wheel. It was as if all the life energy of the great city was
channelled into this spot and hidden away under the ground
for fear of disturbing the "respectable" citizenry. How wrong
first impressions can be was to be shown by later events and
happenings… Soon the cab drove up a side street and I saw a
young man running down a garden path in the miserable night
air stripped to the waist and waving! Being a simple-lifer I much
admired such Spartan fortitude, and I thought such exuberant
behaviour could only come from a raving lunatic or a Soul
brother!

The club itself is in what appears to be an ex-warehouse or
church mission. I like to think it's the latter since it can be said
it is carrying on a tradition of spreading the faith as well as
doubling as a meeting house for the faithful. The lighting is
subdued, but not so dark that you can't see where you are going…
and the dancing is without a doubt the finest I have ever seen
outside of the USA – in fact, I never thought I'd live to see the
day where people could relate the rhythmic content of Soul music
to bodily movement to such a skilled degree in these rigid and
armoured isles!

… As I went to the station to get the train back home, the faint
sounds of Soul music reminded me that the Sunday afternoon
session had already begun, and no matter what obstacles are
placed in its way, Soul music, like life itself, goes on and on.
Because each and every one of us keeps the faith – right on now!'

Extract from a column written by Dave Godin in *Blues & Soul*. June 1970.

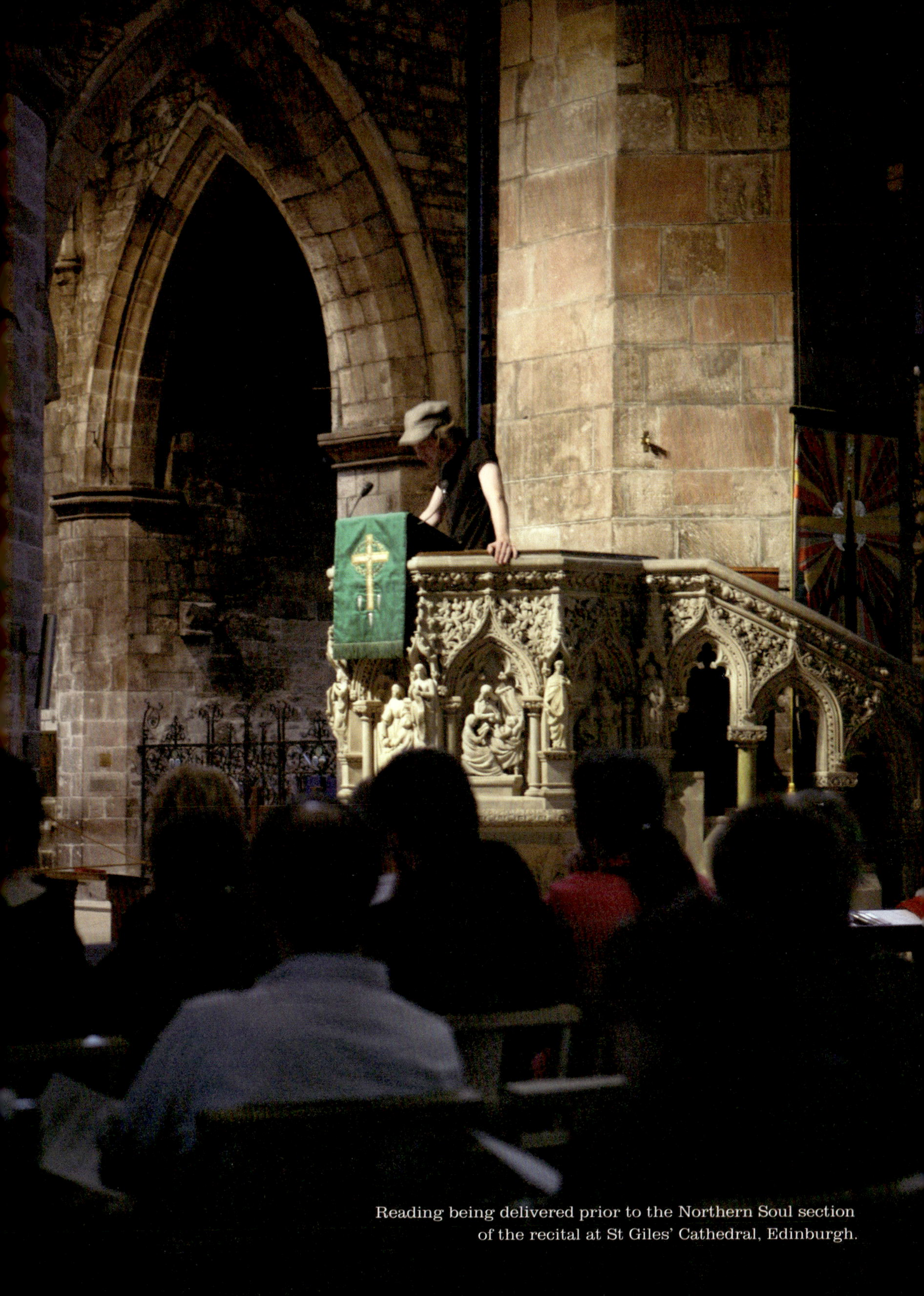

Reading being delivered prior to the Northern Soul section
of the recital at St Giles' Cathedral, Edinburgh.

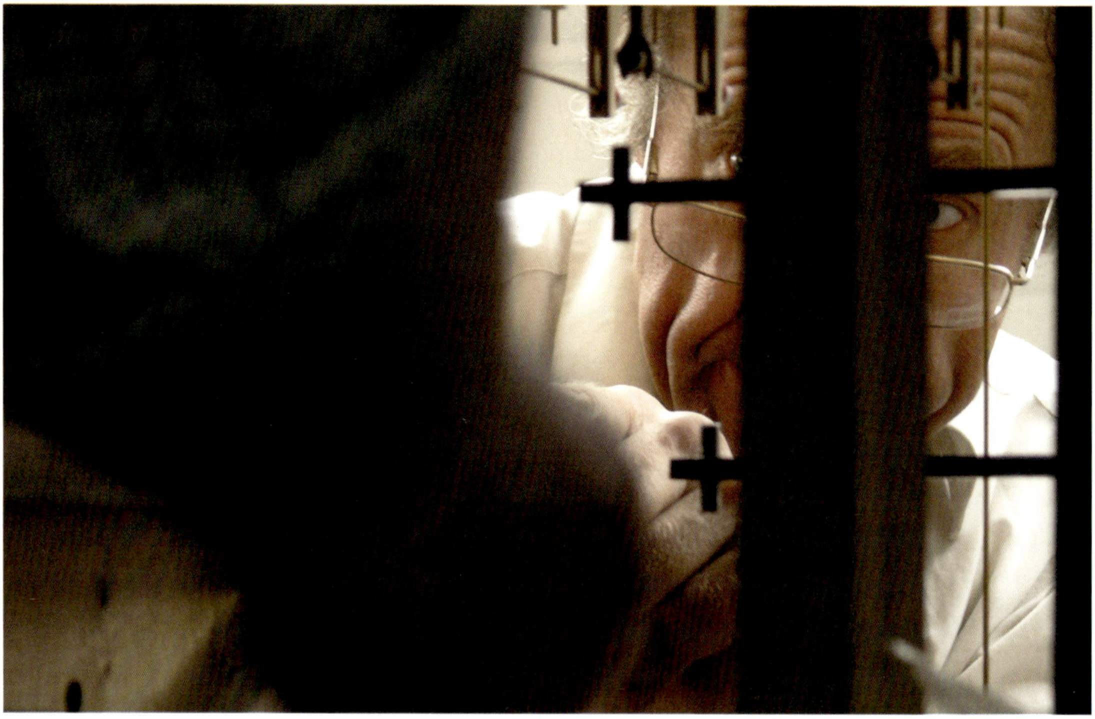

Building of a pipe organ as part of an installation for EAST International, Norwich. 2006.

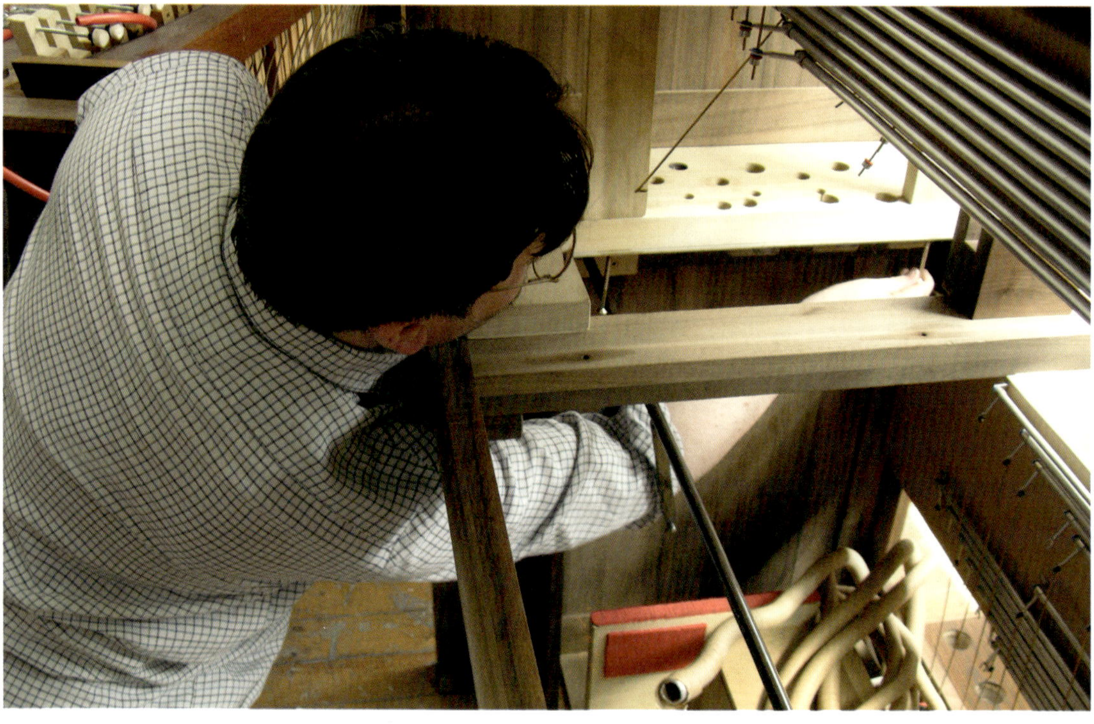

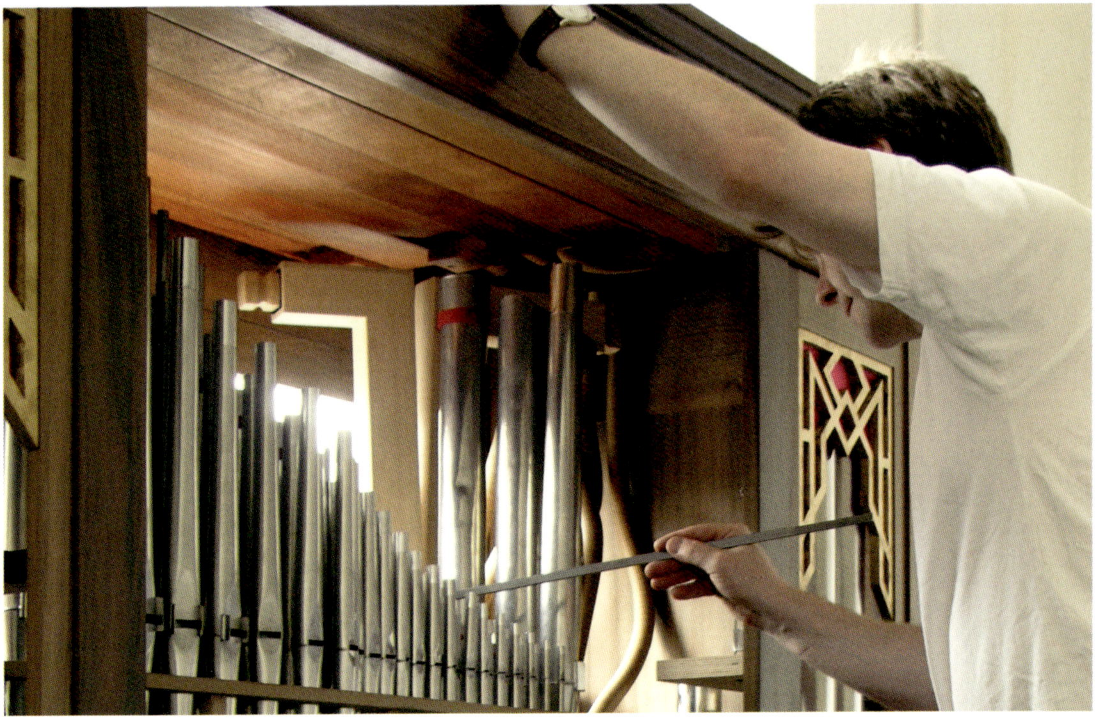

Happy Hardcore recital by organist Paul Ayres for EAST International. 7 July 2006.

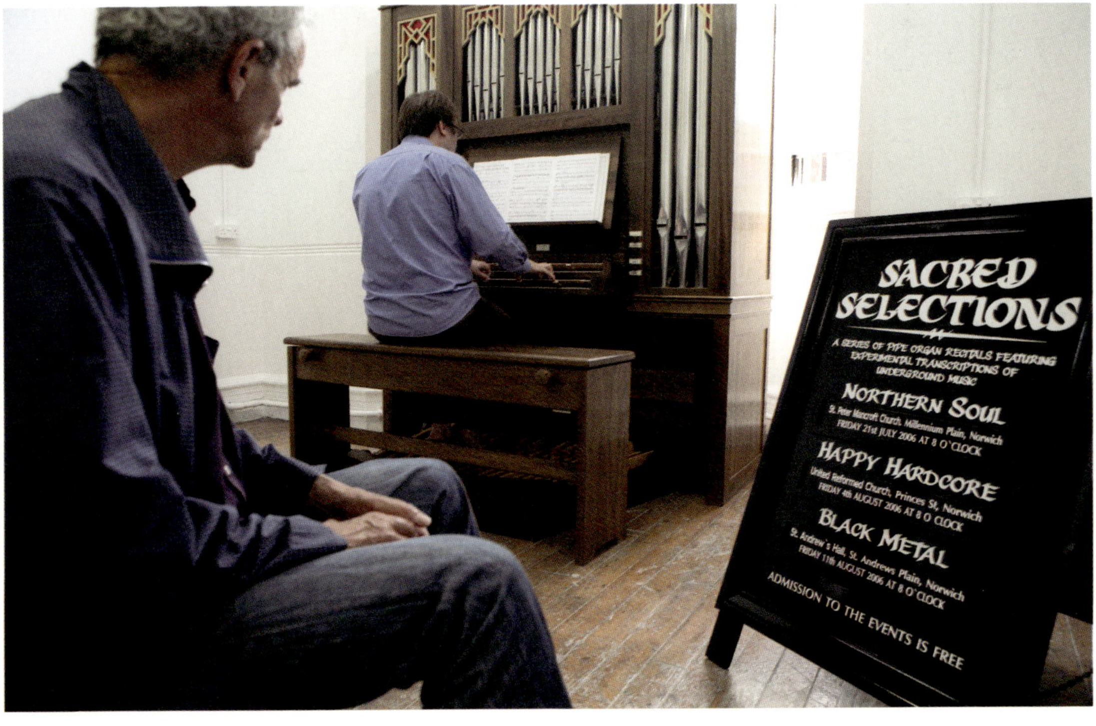

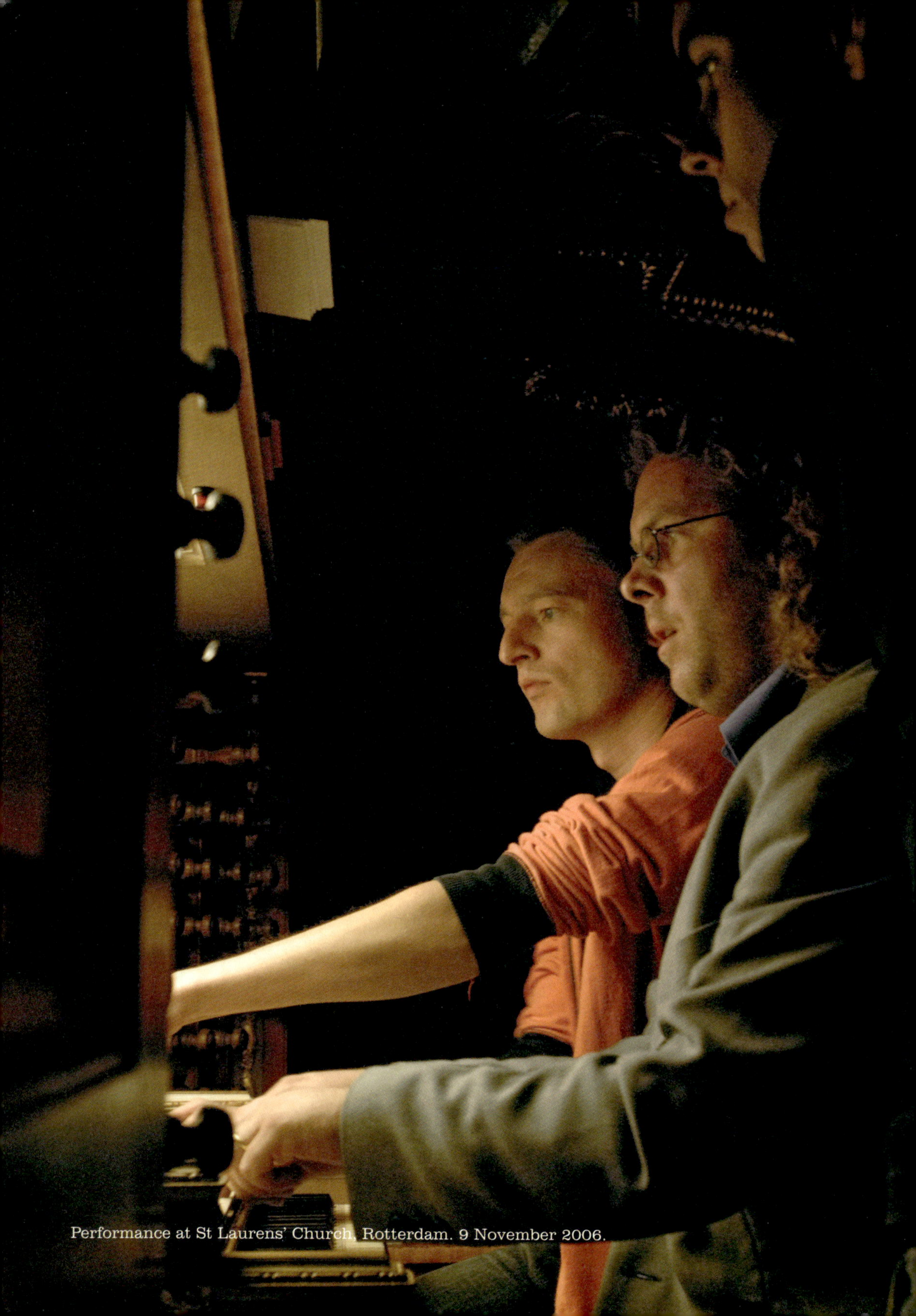

Performance at St Laurens' Church, Rotterdam. 9 November 2006.

Biography

1973   Born in Penzance, Cornwall
1997   Graduated, Newcastle University (BA)

Selected Solo Exhibitions

2007   Kavi Gupta Gallery, Chicago, USA
      [un]promised land, Attitudes espace d'arts contemporains, Geneva, Switzerland
      Ziehersmith, New York, USA
      Lost in the Rhythm, Temple Bar Gallery, Dublin, Ireland
2006   **Solo Project**, NADA Art Fair, Miami, USA
      Pills to Purge Melancholy, Collective Gallery, Edinburgh

Selected Group Exhibitions

2007   **Projection Project II**, Mücsarnok-Kunsthalle, Budapest, Hungary
      Ocho Y Medio, Quito and Maac Cine, Guayaquil, Ecuador
2006   **The Projection Project**, MuHKA, Antwerp, Belgium
      Street: behind the cliché, Witte de With, Rotterdam, Netherlands
      EAST International 06, Norwich Gallery and NSAD, Norwich
      Formal Dining, Hales Gallery, London
      Beck's Futures, ICA, London and off-site venues in Glasgow (CCA)
      and Bristol (Arnolfini)
      Blue Star, Red Wedge, WASPS, Glasgow International, Glasgow
      You Shall Know Our Velocity, BALTIC Centre for Contemporary Art, Gateshead
2005   **Our Surroundings**, Dundee Contemporary Arts, Dundee
      Gatsobyter, Plan 9 Artists Space, Bristol
      Coniston Water Festival, Grizedale Arts, Cumbria
      Everything Must Go, Workplace Gallery, Gateshead
2004   **Romantic Detachment**, PS1 MOMA, New York, USA and Chapter Gallery, Cardiff
      Spark Video International, Forest City Gallery, London, Ontario, Canada
      QSL, FM radio station, MIMA, Middlesbrough
      S1 Salon 'Cabaret', S1 Art Space, Sheffield
2003   **Space Between Us**, Friar House, Newcastle upon Tyne
      Lets Get Married Today!, Grizedale Arts, Cumbria
      Vacant, Reg Vardy Gallery, Sunderland
      Spark International, Spark Contemporary Art Space, Syracuse, USA
      LUX Open, Royal College of Art, London
2002   **Living Proof**, Bewick Court, Newcastle upon Tyne
      Memento, Underground stations on the Tyne and Wear Metro system
      VideoROM, Gian Carla Zanutti Gallery, Milan, Museo Arte Contemporanea,
      Rome and Gallery of Modern Art, Bergamo, Italy
      Mostyn 12 Open, Oriel Mostyn Gallery, Llandudno
      Visions in the Nunnery, Nunnery Gallery, Bow Arts Trust, London
2001   **VideoROM**, Valencia Biennial, Spain

2000   **Small Battles**, Mackey Mayor Building, Manchester
        ROOT, Hull Time Based Arts, Hull
        VANE '00, off-site venue, Newcastle upon Tyne
        NOW Festival, off-site venue, Nottingham
1999   **VANE Export**, Tensta Konsthall, Stockholm, Sweden
        Field, Hallington, Northumberland
        Tongue 'n' Groove, Pine Factory Warehouse, Gateshead
        Inside Out, Adhoc Gallery, Wallsend
1998   **VANE '98**, Live Theatre, Newcastle upon Tyne
1997   **11+11**, Globe Gallery, North Shields
1996   **User Friendly**, off-site venue, Newcastle upon Tyne

Selected Commissions and Residencies

2006   **Socialspaces**, a commission in association with BBC2 and Arts Council England
        Sacred Selections, limited edition CD commissioned by Locus+,
        Newcastle upon Tyne
2002   Grizedale Arts R&D grant awarded in 2002, followed by a residency
        Land and the Samling, residency at Kielder Water and Forest Park,
        Northumberland
2001   **Stretch**, off-site video installation commissioned by Sunderland Arts for the
        project **Retail Therapy**
        Allotment, residency with pigeon fanciers at allotments in Wallsend
2000   **Roll-in' Along**, public video intervention commissioned by Work & Leisure
        International, Manchester

Selected Awards

2006   **Beck's Futures**, awarded by the ICA and Beck's
2003   **RSA Art for Architecture**, supporting a lead artist role with the Tyne and Wear
        Fire and Rescue Service

Collections

National Collecting Scheme for Scotland, McManus Galleries, Dundee
Cherrybrisk Collection, London
Private Collections

Exhibition Catalogues

2006   **Beck's Futures 2006**, published by the ICA. ISBN 1-900300-50-8
        EAST International 2006, published by Norwich Gallery. ISBN 1-872482-80-5
2004   **QSL FM**, published by MIMA. ISBN 0-860830-63-2
        Workplace, published by AEN and Workplace Gallery. ISBN 1-873757-15-8

Unless otherwise stated, exhibitions, commissions and residencies took place in the United Kingdom.

PROGRAMME OF

SACRED SELECTIONS

A SERIES OF PIPE ORGAN RECITALS FEATURING EXPERIMENTAL TRANSCRIPTIONS OF UNDERGROUND MUSIC

'Everywhere throughout Presbyterian Scotland we hear of congregations being sent to worship for a time elsewhere - in order that their regular place of worship may be made into a fixed habitation for an organ. All this expense and trouble, to be put to the divine gift of music to its noblest use in the public service of that Being whose gift it is, are but the outcome of that spirit of liberty in art which not all the dark cobwebs ever spun or yet to be spun by theological spiders can ever hide or repress.'

WRITER UNKNOWN, DUNDEE ADVERTISER, C.1880

ADMISSION TO THE EVENTS IS FREE

- Northern Soul -

St Paul's Church, Bedford Street, Covent Garden
THURSDAY 27TH APRIL 2006, AT 7 O'CLOCK

Music selected by: Ali Duff, Tam McClymont and Alan Watson
Transcribed for the organ by: Andrew Macintosh (Royal College of Organists)
Performed by: Daniel Moult (St Peter's Church, Eaton Square)
and William Whitehead (Royal Academy of Music)

Used to describe the genre of Black American Soul music listened to in hops and small clubs in the north of Britain in the mid 1960s, 'Northern Soul' has become one of the longest running scenes in the history of British music. During the 1970s, obscure records with strong vocals and fast beats packed dance-floors at all-night venues, from the Marryat Hall, Dundee to the legendary Wigan Casino. Despite all odds, Northern Soul has continued to survive, due to the passion of 'Soulies' throughout the UK, and faith in a dance culture that refuses to die.

"YOU DIDN'T SAY A WORD"	...	*... Yvonne Baker*
"TOUCH MY HEART"...		*... The Vonettes*
"NO PART TIME LOVE FOR ME" ...		*... Martha Starr*
"OPEN THE DOOR TO YOUR HEART"		*... Darrell Banks*
"I'M ON MY WAY"		*... Dean Parrish*

❧ EARLIEST RECORDS SHOW THAT WILLIAM GRAY BUILT A THREE MANUAL ORGAN IN ST PAUL'S IN THE LATE 1700S. THE PRESENT INSTRUMENT, BY HENRY BEVINGTON, WAS INSTALLED IN 1861, AND MOST LIKELY INCORPORATED MUCH OF GRAY'S ORGAN AND PARTS FROM THE ORIGINAL CASEWORK DESIGNED BY THOMAS HARDWICK. AS ST PAUL'S WAS AT THAT TIME WAS A COMPARATIVELY POOR CHURCH, NO MAJOR RECONSTRUCTION OF THE ORGAN EVER TOOK PLACE, AND CONSEQUENTLY THE INSTRUMENT STILL RETAINS ITS MECHANICAL ACTION FOR BOTH THE KEYS AND STOP CONTROL.

– Happy Hardcore –

St Matthew's Church, Great Peter Street, Westminster

THURSDAY 4TH MAY 2006, AT 7 O'CLOCK

Music selected by: DJ Sy (Quosh Records)
Transcribed for the organ by: John Riley (St Paul's & St George's Episcopal Church, Edinburgh)
Performed by: Paul Ayres (St George's Church, Hanover Square)

With its mix of celebratory, uplifting tunes based around hectic breakbeats and rapid pace, Happy Hardcore creates an infectious energy that harks back to the golden era of UK Rave. This eclectic choice of anthemic tracks, selected by one of Hardcore's most renowned dj/producers, spans almost a decade - from the memorable riffs of *Midnight Express* by Hopscotch, to the Trance influences of Sy and Demo's *Stay With Me*.

"Shooting Star" … … … … …	*Bang*
"Midnight Express" … … …	*Hopscotch*
"Braveheart" … … …	*Joining of the Clans*
"Stay With Me" … … … …	*Sy & Demo*
"Power Of Love" … … … … …	*Q-Tex*
"Heart Of Gold" … … …	*Force and Styles*

❀ A catastrophic fire at St Matthew's in May 1977 destroyed much of the church and its organ. However the present, much smaller, building is still furnished with many of the original fittings. Mander Organs completed the new organ in September 1989, in a broadly 18th century style. Its position under a single arch, in what is now the nave, was determined following exhaustive acoustical tests. Although just 17 years old, the instrument has already earned a reputation amongst London's finest due to its beauty, clarity and musicality.

- Black Metal -

St Dominic's Priory, Southampton Road, Haverstock Hill

FRIDAY 12TH MAY 2006, AT 8 O'CLOCK

Music selected by: Bruno Frenguelli and Grim Reality
Transcribed for the organ by: Andrew Macintosh (Royal College of Organists)
Performed by: Andrew Macintosh (Royal College of Organists)

Built on the rise of extreme Metal in the 1980s, Black Metal combines demonic lyrics with a brutal musical approach. Tyneside's Thrash pioneers Venom, lay claim to having coined the moniker in 1982 with the release of their album, *Black Metal*. Since then, the genre has expanded beyond its underground roots and proved itself to be one of the most progressive and important additions to the Metal fraternity.

"ALSVARTR (THE OATH)"	*Emperor*
"BLOOD FIRE DEATH"	*Bathory*
"DUSK AND HER EMBRACE"	*Cradle of Filth*
"AT THE HEART OF WINTER"	*Immortal*

IN 1225, THE 'BLACK FRIARS' OF THE DOMINICAN ORDER ESTABLISHED A PRIORY AT LUDGATE FROM WHICH THEY WERE EXPELLED BY ELIZABETH I IN 1559. ALMOST 300 YEARS LATER THE FOUNDATIONS OF THEIR FIRST POST-REFORMATION PRIORY WERE LAID. PLANS WERE PUT BEFORE THE EMINENT ORGAN BUILDER 'FATHER' HENRY WILLIS, WHO PERSONALLY OVERSAW THE COMPLETION OF THE INSTRUMENT FOR THE OPENING OF ST DOMINIC'S IN 1883. TODAY, THE 'PRIORY ORGAN' REMAINS UNALTERED, MAKING IT ONE OF THE MOST HISTORICALLY IMPORTANT INSTRUMENTS OF ITS TYPE IN THE COUNTRY. THE TONAL VARIETY AND IMPRESSIVE IMPACT IN THE BUILDING BEAR TESTAMENT TO WILLIS' EXCEPTIONAL CRAFTSMANSHIP.

With thanks to: Andrew Macintosh, John Riley, Stuart Muir, Ali Duff, Tam McClymont, Alan Watson, Dj Sy, Bruno Frenguelli, Grim Reality, Daniel Moult, William Whitehead, Paul Ayres, Simon Williams, Charles Grant, Simon Gutteridge, Andrew Sampson, Fr Philip Chester and Martin Stacey

Supported by: The Royal College of Organists
Transcriptions commissioned by: Dundee Contemporary Arts
In association with: The Institute of Contemporary Arts